Anti-Inflammatory Cookbook for Beginners 2022

1200 Days of Quick, Easy and Delicious Recipes to Reduce Inflammation, Balance Hormones and Live healthy | Includes a 28-day Weight-Loss Meal Plan

Rosalinda Sherman

Table of Contents

4

Introduction: What is the definition of inflammation?

It is vital to have a strategy when making any type of lifestyle change. Particularly when it comes to food, not having a plan might leave you disappointed and broke. Changing your diet has an impact on several aspects of your life.

If you don't live alone, you will also need to consider your family's nutritional demands, preferences, allergies, finances, and time availability. You'll also need to determine which foods to include and which to exclude from your anti-inflammatory diet. You may effectively create a strategy that clears your route to lower inflammation by incorporating all of this knowledge. Both the synergistic effects of foods ingested in combination and those derived from individual foods contribute to the anti-inflammatory benefits. A person's health can be significantly improved by making even little dietary modifications. Therefore, it's crucial to concentrate on your own goals and make them as attainable as you can.

For instance, adding more fruits or legumes to one's breakfast or lunch might help someone make long-lasting dietary adjustments that will improve their general health and reduce inflammation. However, your diet may need to be changed, as well as the kinds of anti-inflammatory items you should eat, depending on your prior medical history. Before starting this adventure, it would be a good idea to see a dietician.

Since this diet is quite simple, I genuinely believe that starting it doesn't require much contemplation. Simply choose nutritious foods and look for recipes you might like since, just like with any diet, if you don't like it, you won't stick with it for very long. Please bear in mind that perfection is not asked of you. Kiss it and take it gently. By which I mean Keep It Stupid Simple. If you're at a friend's wedding, kindly eat a piece of cake unless you are subject to any kind of medically restricted diet restrictions. Life is too precious to waste; it should be appreciated.

Inflammation is a part of the immune system's reaction to infection or damage. It's the body's method of notifying the immune system that damaged tissues need to be repaired and that germs and viruses must be protected. Infections may quickly spread inside the body without inflammation. Every day, the body experiences acute inflammation from a sore throat or sprained ankle. These are short-term responses that their body experiences to localize the injury or infection. Acute inflammation causes the blood vessels in the afflicted part of the body to enlarge and increase blood flow. White blood cells are the initial line of defense that reach the inflamed region. The infection is contained by white blood cells, which attract other immune system cells. The affected area gets red and swollen in addition to being red since there is so much going on. Inflammation is a process acting as a natural immune response that keeps us alive and healthy. There are two types of inflammation: acute and chronic. Acute inflammation is characterized by a single bout of swelling and discomfort that subsides when the damage heals. Chronic inflammation is a more dangerous disorder that can harm the body's cells and tissues. The hyperactive immune system, which produces cytokines, is the most well-known cause of chronic inflammation. Cytokines are potent molecules that have been related to almost every human illness. Inflammation is the root of many diseases and ailments. Any ailment that ends in "itis" has inflammation: arthritis, endocarditis, appendicitis, bronchitis, colitis, and laryngitis, to name a few. Everyone is affected by inflammation, but those with weakened immune systems, such as children, the elderly, and those with chronic illnesses, are more vulnerable. Fast food items include hamburgers, hotcakes, French fries, and cookies. Processed meats such as canned meats, luncheon meat, bacon, sausages, and bacon products Added sugars, which are included in a variety of sweets, including ice cream, cakes, and doughnuts and go by a variety of names Sweet beverages, such as sugary sodas and pressed fruit juices. Check the food value labels for the following names:

Dextrose, maltose, fructose, honey, table sugar, corn syrup, and honey (and the list goes on)

Seed oils are used in industry. Heavy refinement in mass-produced seed oils has been linked to increased free radicals and inflammation (Fritsch, 2014). These contain many omega6 fatty acids, which in large doses can harm cells and create inflammation.

- Oil from soy
- Canola oil with rapeseed oil
- Oil from corn
- Olive oil

Trans fats are referred to as hydrogenated oils (seed oils that undergo a chemical change to appear in a solid form at room temperature)

Excessive alcohol intake, interacts with your gut microbiota and results in an imbalance that causes inflammatory problems. Refined carbohydrates are foods manufactured from white flour, such as white pasta, white bread, noodles, and white rice. Eat No inflammatory Foods. Anything that is highly processed, excessively fatty, or too sugary should be avoided if you have inflammation. Sweets, cakes, cookies, and soda all lead to weight gain, high blood sugar, and high cholesterol (all of which are associated to inflammation) since they are convenient and low in nutrition.Your body's cytokines, which are inflammatory signals, are released in response to sugar. Soda and other sugary drinks are the main offenders. Experts on anti-inflammatory diets generally advise against consuming additional sugars, such as agave and honey. High fat and processed red meat: If taken in excess, these foods might cause inflammation since they are high in saturated fat.

Saturated fat is now again a problem in foods like butter, whole milk, and cheese.

Instead, eat low fat dairy products. They don't appear to be provocative.

This is because maize oil, safflower oil, and other vegetable oils contain omega6 fatty acids. Naturally, having some omega6 fatty acids would be beneficial, but consuming too much might disturb your body's delicate balance of omega6 and omega3 fatty acids, increasing inflammation.

Margarine, coffee creamers, and other products containing trans fats: Trans fats raise LDL cholesterol and cause inflammation (look for "partially hydrogenated oils" on the label). There is no safe quantity to eat or drink, so refrain.

Barley, rye, and wheat the subject at hand is controversial: gluten. People with celiac disease need to stay away from gluten. The evidence is clear. Nevertheless, whole grains are suitable for the rest of us.

What Are the Consequences of Chronic Inflammation?

When your body is in a condition of chronic inflammation for a long time, it starts to pain. Simply put, what was supposed to save and protect your body from harm now has the opposite effect. As a result, long-term chronic inflammation will cause significant damage to your healthy cells, organs, and tissues. Long-term inflammatory issues are linked to tissue death and DNA damage, as well as the formation of scar tissue, which can be uncomfortable over time.

Acute inflammation, in particular, is a quick reaction to injury or illness. It's also frequently contained in a small region. When it comes to inflammation, there are five cardinal indications to look for: (1) pain, (2) redness, (3) heat, (4) swelling, and (5) loss of function. Inflammation symptoms commonly appear within the first few hours and days after an illness or injury.

While these symptoms may indicate the presence of inflammation, appropriate testing is required to identify inflammation. A medical practitioner must conduct a thorough medical history and physical examination.

In addition, the medical professional must assess for other symptoms, X-rays, and blood testing. According to studies, chronic inflammation has been related to a range of diseases.

Diabetes, heart disease, Alzheimer's disease, and cancer are all considered inflammatory disorders.

The following are some of the diseases linked to inflammation: Heart Disease: Chronic inflammation is a long-term illness that causes plaque to build in the arteries, resulting in heart attacks and strokes. Inflammation may be triggered by a number of factors, the most common of which is poor eating habits. Inflammation can be caused by a variety of factors, including:

Diet: One of the most prevalent causes of inflammation is poor diet.

Animal products, refined carbs such as dairy, red meat, fried meals, refined sugar, baked goods, and highly processed foods are all unhealthy. These meals are connected to saturated or Tran's fat, which causes our bodies to become more inflamed.

Stress: Cortisol chemicals are produced in your body due to stress. These hormones are produced by two adrenal glands. As a result, when you're stressed, your cortisol levels rise. Your immune cells lose their sensitivity as a result of this, which is one of the reasons for inflammation.

Aging: Aging is a normal process in which our body cells replenish, but some cells begin to die. One of the reasons for inflammation is the trash created during this procedure. Aging is an inflammatory process that leads to age related diseases. Alzheimer's disease, type 2 diabetes, cancer, and cardiovascular disease are all diseases that affect the brain.

Sleep disorders: An irregular and poor sleeping pattern have been associated with infection development. As a result of the illness, the sleeping cycle is disrupted, and inflammation rises. Sleep difficulties are linked to most significant diseases and health issues, such as diabetes, high blood pressure, heart attack, and so on.

Obesity: Obesity is linked to inflammation, and gaining weight increases inflammation. Increased inflammation is caused by excess fatty tissue. One of the most efficient strategies to decrease inflammation is to lose weight.

Smoking: One of the high-risk factors for various chronic illnesses is smoking. Tobacco usage can lower your body's ability and diminish the generation of white blood cells. As a result, long term chronic inflammation is one of the primary causes of DNA damage, raising the risk of colon cancer.

Other consequence can be:
- Type 2 diabetes
- Cardiac ailments
- Cancers
- Rheumatoid arthritis
- Asthma
- Neurodegenerative diseases, including dementia
- Inflammatory bowel disease

What Exactly Is an Anti-inflammatory Diet?

The types of food you eat will play a huge role in managing or even avoiding inflammation. Some foods are classified as anti-inflammatory substances and will help fight inflammation. Such food will be high in the following commodities:

Polyphenols Antioxidants Omega3 essential oils Fiber

Eating well isn't as difficult as you might think. Along with all of the "convenient" readytoeat unhealthy meals, there are items that may be combined to make a quick and nutritious dinner.

Foods That Can Help You Fight Inflammation

Several foods can reduce inflammation. They provide an alternative to pharmaceuticals; hence, adopting an anti-inflammatory diet will benefit your general health. The most excellent method to improve your happiness, mental wellbeing, and cognitive health is to eat a balance of healthy grains, complex carbohydrates, and fresh veggies. These are the fundamental considerations in developing the dishes in The Anti-inflammatory Diet Cookbook. The following food kinds should ideally be included in your pantry:

- Organic/fresh vegetables
- Collard greens, kale and spinach
- Broccoli, tomatoes, carrots, peppers, cauliflower
- Sweet potatoes
- Artichokes
- Beans, such as kidney beans, red beans, black beans, and pinto beans
- Healthy fats
- Avocados
- Coconuts
- Olive oil
- Nut butter (almond, hazelnut, coconut)
- Grass-fed meat
- Fatty fish, such as tuna, mackerel, and salmon. Try to choose wild caught fish, and not the farmed variety, if possible
- Free-range, pastured, and organic eggs
- Nuts, like almonds, pistachios, walnuts, and pecans
- Fruits, like cherries, grapes, oranges, apples, blackberries, strawberries and raspberries
- Lentils and pulses for protein

Anti-inflammatory qualities are abundant in many household components. One of the most natural and efficient ways to decrease inflammation is to use home remedies. One of the most effective strategies to combat these diseases is to eat an anti-inflammatory diet. Natural anti-inflammatories can be found in the following kitchen items.

Turmeric: Turmeric is a beautiful spice that can be found in almost any kitchen and has therapeutic benefits. It has been used for ages to cure infections, wounds, liver illness, and the common cold as one of the most refined anti-inflammatory foods. Curcumin is one of the turmeric chemicals that helps decrease inflammation, according to research and studies. Ginger: Ginger has long been used as a traditional medicine to treat various ailments, including nausea, headaches, and infections. It's available in the market as a powder or raw root. It helps relieve muscular discomfort and is particularly useful for arthritis because of its anti-inflammatory effects.

Garlic: Garlic has a strong flavor and is antibacterial and anti-inflammatory in nature. Garlic is beneficial to your health as well as adds taste to your diet. Garlic is one of the recognized anti-inflammatory compounds that can help with arthritic symptoms, according to the study. Clove: Another spice with a strong perfume is clove. It's easy to find in any kitchen. Antibacterial and anti-inflammatory effects are found in cloves. It also has therapeutic characteristics and has been used to heal oral problems for millennia. It also helps manage blood sugar levels in those with type 2 diabetes. To enhance the flavor of your cuisine, you may use it whole or in powder form.

Black pepper: The king of spices, black pepper is high in antioxidants, anti-inflammatory, and antibacterial qualities. According to the study and research, black peppers, which contain a lot of the chemical piperine, are helpful when acute inflammation is still in its early stages.

Breakfasts

Avocado Egg

Prep Time: 5 minutes **Cooking Time**: 20 minutes **Servings**: 4

Ingredients:
2 ripe avocados
4 eggs
Salt and pepper to taste

Directions:
Heat your oven to 350 degrees Fahrenheit. A 6cup muffin tray should be lightly oiled and set aside. Mix the eggs, almond milk, and basil in a medium dish until foamy. Add the scallion, broccoli, and spinach by stirring. Put prepared egg mixture into muffin tins by spoonfuls. The frittatas must bake for about 20 minutes until they are puffy, golden, and fully cooked. Serve after seasoning with black pepper and sea salt.

NUTRITION: Calories: 290Total Fat: 24gSaturated Fat: 3gTotal Carbs: 10gNet Carbs: 3g Protein: 11gSugar: 1gFiber: 7g Sodium: 109mgPotassium 428mg

Coconut Pancakes

Prep Time: 10 minutes. **Cooking time**: 5 minutes per pancake. **Servings**: 2

Ingredients:
½ cup coconut, plus additional as needed
½ tablespoon maple syrup
¼ cup coconut flour
½ teaspoon salt
2 eggs
½ tablespoon coconut oil or almond butter, plus additional for greasing the pan
½ teaspoon vanilla extract
½ teaspoon baking soda

Directions:
Using an electric mixer, combine coconut milk, maple syrup, eggs, coconut oil, and vanilla in a medium bowl.
Combine the baking soda, coconut flour, and salt in a shallow mixing bowl. Set the dry ingredients with the wet ingredients in a mixing bowl and beat until smooth and lumpfree.
If the batter is too dense, add more liquid to thin it down to a typical pancake batter consistency.
Using coconut oil, lightly grease a big skillet or pan. Preheat the oven to mediumhigh.

Cook until golden brown on the rim. Cook for another 2 minutes.
Continue to cook the leftover batter while stacking the pancake on a tray.

NUTRITION: Calories: 193 Total fat: 11 g Total carbohydrates: 15 g Sugar: 6 g Fiber: 6 g Protein: 9 g Sodium: 737 mg

Anti-Inflammatory Crepes

Prep Time: 5 minutes **Cooking Time**: 4 minutes **Servings**: 4

Ingredients:
2 tablespoon coconut flour
4 large eggs, pastureraised
1 tablespoon coconut oil
1 cup hazelnuts, soaked in water overnight
2/3 cup dark chocolates
½ teaspoon vanilla extract
2 tablespoon maple syrup
½ cup water

Directions:
 Preheat the oven to 3500F.
 In a bowl, mix the coconut flour, eggs, and water until wellcombined.
 Heat oil in a skillet over medium flame and grease the skillet with coconut oil.
 Scoop 1/3 cup of the crepe mixture into the skillet and cook for 4
minutes while flipping halfway through the cooking time.
 Repeat until all batter is made into crepes.
 Make the hazelnut sauce by combining the hazelnuts, dark chocolates, vanilla extract, and maple syrup in a blender.
 Pulse until smooth.
 Spread the Nutella sauce over the crepes before serving.

NUTRITION: Calories: 465Total Fat: 29gSaturated Fat: 6gTotal Carbs: 46gNet Carbs: g Protein: 9gSugar: 32gFiber: 5g Sodium: 53mgPotassium 401mg

Raspberry Oatmeal Bars

Prep Time:5 minutes. **Cook time** 15 minutes. **Serves**: 6

Ingredients:
3 cups steel cut oats
3 large eggs
2 cups vanilla almond milk, unsweetened
⅓ cup erythritol
1 teaspoon pure vanilla extract
¼ teaspoon salt
1 cup frozen raspberries

Directions:
In a suitable bowl, mix together all the recipe ingredients except the berries.
Fold in berries.

Layer a 6" cake pan with cooking oil. Transfer the prepared berry oat mixture to this pan and cover this pan with aluminum foil.

Pour 1 cup water into the instant pot and set the steam rack inside.

Place this pan with the oat mixture on top of the rack. Close the lid and secure it well.

Pressure cook for 15 minutes.

When done, release the pressure quickly until the float valve drops and then unlock lid.

Carefully remove this pan from the insert of the Instant pot and remove the foil.

Let it cool down before cutting into bars and serving.

NUTRITION: Calories 236; Fat 2g; Sodium 135mg; Carbs 39g; Fiber 6g; Sugars 8g; Protein 8g

Wonderful Breakfast Salad with Grapefruit and Berries

Servings: 2 **Cooking Time**: 0 Minute

Ingredients:

1 cup oats, steel cut

1 pink grapefruit, peeled and sliced

2 oranges, peeled and sliced

454 g low fat Greek yogurt

handful of cranberries or cherries, fresh

Directions:

Mix the oats and fruit with the yogurt. Allow to soak overnight.

Serve and top with honey and cranberries or cherries. The oats should be nice and mushy and will soaked up the flavors of the fruit.

NUTRITION: Per Serving: Calories: 302 ;Fat: 7g ;Protein: 21g ;Carbs: 58g .

Sweet Pancake with Almond, Apricot, Peach And Greek Yogurt

Servings: 2 **Cooking Time**: 4 Minutes

Ingredients:

$^1/_3$ cup buckwheat, banana or almond meal flour 1 free range eggs

½ cup almond, hazelnut or soya milk

½ teaspoon baking powder, glutenfree

1 apricot, peeled and cubed

1 peach, peeled and cubed

1 teaspoon vanilla extract

1 tablespoon low fat Greek yogurt

1 teaspoon coconut oil

Directions:

Preheat the oven on low.

Whisk all the ingredients except from the Greek yogurt until light and fluffy.

Leave to one side.

Heat coconut oil over a medium heat in a pan.

Pour ¼ of the mixture into a pancake shape and cook for 30 seconds to a minute.

Flip and repeat.

Stack on a plate. Keep it warm in an oven on a low heat.

Repeat until you've used all of the mixture.
Serve with a dollop of Greek yogurt and extra fruit if preferred.
Keep the extra in a sealed container in the fridge for 23 days.

NUTRITION: Per Serving: Calories: 75 ;Fat: 3g ;Protein: 2g ;Carbs: 11g .

Salmon Egg Scrambled

Prep Time: 10 minutes **Cooking Time**: 8 minutes **Serve**: 2

Ingredients:
4 eggs
2 tbsp unsweetened almond milk
4 smoked salmon slices, chopped
1 tbsp olive oil
1 tbsp fresh chives, chopped
Pepper
Salt

Directions:
Heat olive oil in a pan over medium heat.
Whisk eggs with milk, chives, pepper, and salt in a bowl.
Pour egg mixture into the pan and cook over mediumlow heat. Stir constantly.
When eggs start to set, add salmon slices and cook for 12 minutes.
Serve and enjoy.

NUTRITION: Calories 388 Fat 23 g Carbohydrates 0.9 g Sugar 0.7 g Protein 43 g Cholesterol 366 mg

Strawberry & Pecan Breakfast

Servings: 2 Cooking Time: 15 Minutes

Ingredients:
1 can coconut milk, refrigerated overnight 1 cup granola
½ cup pecans, chopped
1 cup sliced strawberries
Directions:

Drain the coconut milk liquid. Layer the coconut milk solids, granola, and strawberries in small glasses.
Top with chopped pecans and serve right away.
NUTRITION: Per Serving: Calories: 644;Fat: 79g;Protein: 23g;Carbs: 82g.

Beef Breakfast

Prep Time: 20 minutes.   **Cook time:** 20 minutes.   **Serves:** 4

Ingredients:
1 tablespoon olive oil
1 pound lean ground beef
2 teaspoons bottled minced garlic
2 cups chopped cauliflower
1 cup diced carrots

1 zucchini, diced
2 scallions, white and green parts, chopped
Sea salt
Black pepper
2 tablespoons chopped fresh parsley

Directions:
Place a suitable skillet over medium high heat and add the olive oil.
Add the ground beef and garlic. Sauté for almost 8 minutes until cooked through.
Stir in the cauliflower, carrots, and zucchini. Sauté for almost 10 minutes until tender.
Stir in the scallions and sauté for almost 1 minute more.
Season the prepared mixture with black pepper and sea salt. Serve topped with the parsley.

NUTRITION :Calories 277; Fat 7g; Sodium 115mg; Carbs 8g; Fiber 7g; Sugars 6g; Protein 34g

Papaya Breakfast Boat

Prep Time: 5 minutes **Cooking time:** 0 minutes **Servings:** 2

You day starts with a healthy digestive system, and papaya boats are full of fiber, vitamins and enzymes to keep you healthy from the inside out.

Ingredients
1 papaya, cut lengthwise in half, and seeds removed 1 C. yogurt, unsweetened
1 lime, zested
3 tbsp. raw oats
1 tbsp. coconut, unsweetened, shredded
½ banana, sliced
¼ C. raspberries
1 tbsp. walnuts, chopped
1 tsp. chia seeds
1 tsp. raw honey

Directions:
Place papaya halves on plates and place yogurt on top of each.
Then, top each half with lime zest, oats, coconut, banana, raspberries, walnuts, chia seeds.
Drizzle with honey and serve.

NUTRITION: Calories: 315 kcal Carbohydrates: 50 g Protein: 4 g
Fat: 13 g Sodium: 749 mg Fiber: 4 g Sugar: 235 g

Root Vegetable Egg Casserole

Prep Time: 12minutes **Total Time:** 45minutes **Yield: g**

Ingredients:
1 tbsp. avocado oil
1 small yellow onion, peeled and diced
1 small turnip, peeled and diced 1 medium parsnip, peeled and diced 2 small carrots, peeled and
1 tsp. kosher Salt diced
8 large eggs

1 tbsp. lemon juice
1 tbsp. fresh thyme leaves

Directions:

To the inner pot, add in oil and allow to Sauté for 1 minute. Add the onion, turnip, parsnip, carrots, and Salt. Cook until the vegetables are softened, 10minutes. Press the Cancel button. In a bowl, add the lemon juice and eggs.

Add the thyme and vegetable mixture and stir to combine. Spray the inside of a 7cup glass bowl with cooking spray. Transfer the egg mixture to the bowl.

To your inner pot, add a cup of and set the steam rack inside. Set your bowl on the steam rack. Secure the lid. Pressure cook for about 18minutes. Quick release pressure and unlock the lid. Set bowl aside and let cool for 5minutes before slicing and serving.

NUTRITION: Calories: 221 Fat: 12g Protein: 14g Fiber: 3g Carbs: 12g Sugar: 3g

Walnut and Banana Bowl

Prep Time: 13minutes   **Total Time:** 30minutes   **Yield:** 4

Ingredients:

2 c. water
1 c. steel cut
oats
1 c. almond milk
1 tsp. vanilla
flavoring
¼ c. walnuts,
2 tbsps. chia
chopped
seeds
2 bananas

Directions:

Toss all ingredients in a pot. Cook on simmer over medium high heat for about 15minutes. Serve and enjoy!

NUTRITION: Calories: 162 Fat: 4g Carbohydrates: 11g Protein: 4g

Sweet Potato Oat Bars

Servings: 6 **Cooking Time:** 35 Minutes

Ingredients:

Sweet potato, cooked, mashed
1 cup Almond milk, unsweetened
0.75 cups of Egg
1 Date paste
5 tablespoons Vanilla extract
5 teaspoons Baking soda
1 teaspoon Cinnamon, ground
1 teaspoon Cloves, ground

0.25 teaspoon Nutmeg, ground
0.5 teaspoon Ginger, ground
0.5 teaspoon Flaxseed, ground
2 tablespoons Protein powder
1 serving Coconut flour
0.25 cup Oat flour
1 cup Dried coconut, unsweetened
0.25 cup Pecans, chopped
0.25 cup

Directions:

Warm the oven to Fahrenheit 375 degrees and line a square eightbyeight inch baking dish with kitchen parchment. You want to leave some parchment paper hanging over the sides of the pan for lifting once the bars are done baking.

Into your stand blender, add all of the ingredients for the sweet potato oat bars except for the dried coconut and chopped pecans. Allow the mixture to pulse for a few moments until the mixture is smooth and then stop the blender. You may need to scrape the sides of the blender down and then blend again.

Pour the coconut and pecans into the batter and then stir them in with a spatula.

Do not blend the mixture again, as you don't want these pieces blended. Pour the sweet potato oat bar mixture into your prepared pan and spread it out.

Place your sweet potato oat bar dish in the middle of your oven and allow it to bake until the bars are set through, about twentytwo to twentyfive minutes.

Remove the pan from the oven. Set a wire cooling rack next to the baking dish and then gently lift the kitchen parchment by the overhang and carefully lift it from the dish and onto the wire rack to cool. Allow the sweet potato oat bars to cool completely before slicing.

NUTRITION: Calories: 248 Cal Fat: 14 g Fiber: 4 g Carbs: 10 g Protein: 14 g

Eggs With Cheese

Servings: 1   Cooking times: 6 minutes

Ingredients:
¼ c. chopped tomato
1 egg white
1 chopped green onion
2 tablespoons Fat free milk
1 slice of whole wheat bread
1 egg
½ oz. reduced fat grated cheddar cheese

Directions:
Mix the egg and egg whites in a bowl and add the milk.
Scramble the mixture in a non-stick frying pan until the eggs cook.
Meanwhile, toast the bread.
Spoon the scrambled egg mixture onto the toasted bread and top with the cheese until it melts.
Add the onion and the tomato.

NUTRITION: Calories: 251, Fat:10 g, Carbs:23 g, Protein:19 g, Sugars:8 g, Sodium:451 mg

Milk and Creamy Yogurt Bowl

Prep Time: 10 minutes   **Cook time:** 10 minutes   **Serves** 1

Ingredients:

1 tablespoon heavy whipping cream
½ cup plain whole milk Greek yogurt
1 tablespoon unsweetened pumpkin puree
1 teaspoon pumpkin pie spice (no sugar added)
1 to 2 teaspoons monk fruit extract or sugarfree sweetener (optional) ½ teaspoon vanilla extract
2 tablespoons coarsely chopped pecans

Directions:

In a small bowl, using an immersion blender or whisk, whisk the cream for 2 to 3 minutes, until thick and doubled in volume. Set aside.

In a medium bowl, mix together the yogurt, pumpkin, pumpkin pie spice, sweetener (if using), and vanilla.

Top the yogurt mixture with the pecans and whipped cream and serve.

NUTRITION: Calories: 266   Fat:20g   Protein: 13g   Total Carbs: 9g Fiber: 2g Net Carbs: 7g

A Quick antipasto pasta

Prep Time: 10 minutes **Cooking Time**: 15 minutes **Servings**: 1

Ingredients:

300g farfalle pasta
1/3 cup basil leaves
1/4 cup (40g) pine nuts, toasted
1/4 cup (20g) finely grated parmesan
1 garlic clove, crushed
120g pkt Coles Australian Baby Rocket
1/2 cup (125ml) olive oil
100g thickly sliced Don Ham on the Bone from the Deli, torn 50g slices Coles Deli Herb Coated Salami, chopped
100g Coles Danish Fetta, coarsely crumbled
140g Coles Deli Giant Pitted Kalamata Olives, halved
170g Coles Deli Semi Dried Tomatoes with Fresh Basil, coarsely chopped

Directions:

Cook the pasta in a large pot of boiling water according to the package recommendations, or until al dente. Drain well, saving 12 cups (125ml)
of the cooking liquid. Then, reintroduce the spaghetti to the pan.
Meanwhile, combine the basil, pine nuts, parmesan, garlic, and half of the rocket in a food processor and process until finely chopped. While the engine is running, pour the oil in a thin, steady stream until well blended. Season.
Combine the pesto, ham, salami, feta, olive, tomato, leftover cooking liquid, and remaining rocket in the pan with the noodles. Toss gently to blend. Distribute the pasta mixture among the serving dishes. Serve right away.

Orange Oatmeal Muffins

Prep Time:7 minutes.   **Cook time:** 15 minutes.   **Serves:** 6

Ingredients:
3 cups old fashioned rolled oats
1 teaspoon baking powder
¼ teaspoon salt
1 teaspoon ground cinnamon
¼ cup vanilla almond milk, unsweetened
¼ cup fresh orange juice
3 ⅓ cups mashed bananas
1 large egg
¼ cup erythritol

Directions:
In a suitable bowl, mix all of the ingredients together, while stirring until well combined.
Place six silicone muffin cups inside of a 6" cake pan. Spoon the oatmeal mixture into the muffin cups. Cover this pan with aluminium foil.
Pour 1 cup water into the insert of the Instant Pot and set the steam rack inside. Set the cake pan with the muffins on the rack. Close the lid and secure it well.
Pressure cook for 15 minutes.
When cooked, release the pressure quickly until the float valve drops and then unlock lid.
Carefully remove this pan from the insert of the Instant pot and remove the foil from the top. Let the muffins cool 15 minutes before eating. They will become firmer as they cool.

NUTRITION: Calories 148; Fat 5g; Sodium 117mg; Carbs 29g; Fiber 8g; Sugars 5g; Protein 5g

Coconut Rice with Berries

Prep Time: 10 minutes. **Cooking time**: 30 minutes. **Servings**: 2

Ingredients:
¾ cup water
¾ teaspoon salt
½ cup fresh blueberries, or raspberries, divided ½ cup shaved coconut, divided
½ cup brown basmati rice
½ cup coconut milk
2 pitted and chopped dates
¼ cup toasted slivered almonds, divided

Directions:
 Combine the water, basmati rice, coconut milk, spice, and date pieces in a medium saucepan over high heat.
 Stir constantly until the mixture boils. Set the heat to low and cook, occasionally stirring, for 20 to 30 minutes, or until the rice is tender.
 Place some blueberries, almonds, and coconut on top of each serving of rice.

Blueberry Breakfast Blend

Prep Time: 8 minutes. **Cooking time**: 0 minutes. **Servings**: 1

Ingredients:
$1/3$ teaspoon turmeric
½ cup spinach
¾ cup fresh blueberries
1 cup fresh pineapple chunks
1 cup water
1 tablespoon chia seeds
1 tablespoon lemon juice

Directions:
Combine all the ingredients in your blender. Blend to a smooth consistency.

NUTRITION: Calories: 260 Fat: 6 g Protein: 13 g Sodium: 30 mg Total carbs: 35 g

Golden Milk

Prep Time: 5 Minutes **Cooking Time**: 5 Minutes **Servings**: 2

Ingredients:
1 tbsp. Coconut Oil
1 ½ cups Coconut Milk, light
Pinch of Pepper
1 ½ cups Almond Milk, unsweetened
¼ tsp. Ginger, grated
1 ½ tsp. Turmeric, grounded
¼ tsp. Cinnamon, grounded
Sweetener of your choice, as needed

Directions:
To make this healthy beverage, you need to place all the ingredients in a mediumsized saucepan and mix it well.
After that, heat it over medium heat for 3 to 4 minutes or until it is hot but not boiling. Stir continuously.
Taste for seasoning. Add more sweetener or spice as required by you.
Finally, transfer the milk to the serving glass and enjoy it.
Tip: Instead of cinnamon powder, you can also use the cinnamon stick, which can be discarded at the end if you prefer a much more intense flavor.

NUTRITION: Calories: 205Kcal Proteins: 2g Carbohydrates: 9g Fat: 15g

Spiced Morning Chia Pudding

Prep Time: 10 Minutes **Cooking Time**: 5 Minutes **Servings**: 1

Ingredients:
½ tsp. Cinnamon
1 ½ cups Cashew Milk
1/8 tsp. Cardamom, grounded
1/3 cup Chia Seeds

1/8 tsp. Cloves, grounded
2 tbsp. Maple Syrup
1 tsp. Turmeric

Directions:
To begin with, combine all the ingredients in a medium bowl until well mixed.
Next, spoon the mixture into a container and allow it to sit overnight.
In the morning, transfer to a cup and serve with toppings of your choice.
Tip: You can top it with toppings of your choice like coconut flakes or seeds etc.

NUTRITION: Calories: 237Kcal Proteins: 1g Carbohydrates: 29g Fat: 1g

Milk and Garlic Meatloaves

Prep Time: 10 minutes   **Cook time**: 30 minutes   **Serves** 2

Ingredients:
½ cup lean ground turkey
½ cup skinless ground chicken
¼ cup coconut milk
1 minced garlic clove
¼ cup chives, finely chopped
1 tablespoon paprika
Sprinkle of chopped parsley
Sprinkle of black pepper
1 teaspoon coconut oil

Directions:
Preheat the oven to 400°f/200°C/Gas Mark
Mix turkey, chicken, garlic, chives, paprika, and coconut milk together, mixing until the ingredients hold.
Season with black pepper to taste.
Line a muffin tin with coconut oil and divide the mixture into each hole.
Bake in the oven for 30 minutes or until the meat is cooked through.
Sprinkle cooked meatloaves with parsley and serve alone or with side salad.

NUTRITION: Calories: 607   Fat: 44g   Protein: 45g   Total Carbs: 6g   Fiber: 3g   Net Carbs: 3g

Breakfast and Brunch Mushroom Crepes

Servings: 4 **Cooking Time**: 25 Minutes

Ingredients:
1 cup wholewheat flour
1 tsp onion powder
½ tsp baking soda
¼ tsp sea salt
1 cup crumbled tofu
⅓ cup almond milk
¼ cup lemon juice
2 tbsp extravirgin olive oil

½ cup chopped mushrooms
½ cup finely chopped onion
2 cups collard greens

Directions:
Combine the flour, onion powder, baking soda, and salt in a bowl.
Place the tofu, almond milk, lemon juice, and oil in your food processor. Blitz until everything is well combined. Add to the the flour mixture and mix to combine. Stir in mushrooms, onion, and collard greens.
Heat a skillet and grease with cooking spray. Lower the heat and spread a ladleful of the batter across the surface of the skillet. Cook for 4 minutes on both sides or until set. Remove to a plate. Repeat the process until no batter is left, greasing with a little more oil, if needed.
Serve.

NUTRITION: Per Serving: Calories: 282;Fat: 15g;Protein: 10g;Carbs: 30g.

Fruit and Millet Breakfast

Prep Time: 30 minutes **Cooking time**: 15 minutes **Servings**: 2

Millet is a super grain full of nutrients and, when combined with fruits, makes a wholesome breakfast for anyone.

Ingredients:
½ C. millet
1 C. water
2 tbsp. raisins
1 tbsp. currants
⅛ tsp. cinnamon
⅛ tsp. vanilla extract
1 C. coconut milk, unsweetened and divided
1 tsp. honey
½ C. raspberries
½ C. blueberries
1 tsp. hemp hearts
1 tsp. chia seeds
1 tsp. mint, chopped

Directions:
Place millet and water in a medium saucepan over medium heat.
Bring to a boil, and then add the raisins, currants, cinnamon, and vanilla.
Cover with a lid, reduce heat to low, and let it cook for another 10 minutes until liquid is absorbed.
Turn heat off and let sit for 11 minutes.
Add coconut milk, honey, raspberries, blueberries, hemp hearts, and chia seeds. Turn heat to low and let cook for 2 minutes.
Transfer to bowls and garnish with mint.

NUTRITION: Calories: 565 kcal Carbs: 64 g Protein: 10 g Fat: 35 g Fiber: 98

Healthy Chia Pudding

Prep Time: 10 minutes **Cooking Time**: 5 minutes **Serve**: 2

Ingredients:
6 tbsp chia seeds
1 tbsp maple syrup
¼ tsp ground ginger
¼ tsp ground cinnamon
1 ¼ tsp turmeric
2 cups can coconut milk
1/8 tsp ground black pepper

Directions:
Add milk, turmeric, cinnamon, cardamom, ginger, maple syrup, and black pepper into the glass jar and stir until well combined.
Add chia seeds and stir well. Cover jar with lid and place in the fridge for overnight.
Stir well and serve.

NUTRITION:
Calories 892 Fat 75 g Carbohydrates 50.4 g Sugar 6 g Protein 18 g Cholesterol 0 mg

Breakfast Porridge

Prep Time: 10 minutes **Cooking time**: 50 minutes **Servings**: 2

If you like eating something heavy in the mornings, this is for you. It is light but filling, and packed with essential macronutrients for the day.

Ingredients:
½ C. red or wild rice
½ C. steelcut oats
¼ C. pearl barley
1 cinnamon stick
1–2 tbsp. Splenda
¼ tsp. salt
¼ C. fruit, dried (cranberries, cherries, raisins) Nuts, chopped, maple syrup and/or milk, for serving (optional)

Directions:
Soak rice, barley, farina, and oats in 5 C. of water in a rice cooker.
Add cinnamon stick, Splenda, orange peel, salt, and dried fruit.
Cover the cooker and cook for 50 minutes on 'manual' function.
Serve with nuts on top as desired.

NUTRITION: Calories: 4037 kcal Total Fat: 19 g Saturated Fat: 0.32 g Cholesterol: 0 mg Sodium: 328 mg Carbohydrates: 893 g Fiber: 14 g Sugar: 52 g Protein: 3 g

Lunch

LemonHerb Sardine Salad

Prep Time: 10 minutes **Cooking Time**: 5 minutes **Servings**: 2

Ingredients:

Two 4oz cans oliveoilpacked (drained) sardines Coarse salt and freshly ground black pepper
Great Value Salt, 26 oz
1 tablespoon rinsed capers
2 tablespoons chopped fresh parsley
1 tablespoon chopped fresh tarragon
2 finely diced stalks celery
2 tablespoons extravirgin olive oil
1 teaspoon grated lemon zest
Juice of 1 lemon
1 teaspoon Dijon mustard
Lettuce, for serving

Directions:

In a pan, mix butter, lemon zest, water, mustard, capers, parsley, tarragon, and celery.
Fold gently in sardines and use salt and pepper to season. Serve with lettuce.

NUTRITION: Calories: 160Fat: 22g Sodium: 35mgCarbohydrates: 12gFiber: 13gSugar: 2g Protein: 16g

Grilled Chicken

Prep Time: 10 minutes **Cooking Time**: 10 minutes **Serve**: 4

Ingredients:

1 ½ lbs chicken breasts, skinless & boneless 2 tbsp butter, melted
¼ tsp ground coriander
2 garlic cloves, minced
½ tsp turmeric
¼ tsp paprika
2 tbsp canola oil
½ tsp chili powder
3 tbsp fresh lemon juice
Pepper
Salt

Directions:

Add chicken and remaining ingredients into the ziplock bag, seal bag, and place overnight in the refrigerator.
Preheat the grill.
Place marinated chicken onto the hot grill and cook for 45 minutes on each side.
Serve and enjoy.

NUTRITION: Calories 402 Fat 28 g Carbohydrates 8 g Sugar 0.6 g Protein 46 g Cholesterol 145 mg

Green Soup

Prep Time: 10minutes   **Total time**: 15minutes   **Yield**: 2servings

Ingredients:
1 c. Water
1 c. Spinach, fresh & packed
½ of 1 Lemon,
1 Zucchini, small peeled & chopped
2 tbsp. Parsley,
1 Celery Stalk, fresh & chopped Sea Salt & Black ½ of 1 Avocado, Pepper, as ripe needed
¼ c. Basil
2 tbsp. Chia Seeds
1 Garlic clove, minced

Directions:
To make this easy blended soup, place all the ingredients in a highspeed blender and blend for 3minutes or until smooth. Next, you can serve it cold or warm it up on low heat for a few minutes.

NUTRITION: Calories: 250Proteins: 9g Carbohydrates: 14gFat: 11g

Chicken Breasts and Mushrooms

Prep Time: 5minutes   **Total time**: 30minutes   **Yield**: 6servings

Ingredients:
3 lbs. chicken breasts, skinless and
1 yellow onion, chopped
boneless
1 garlic clove, minced
A pinch of salt and black
pepper
10 mushrooms, chopped
1 tbsp. olive oil
2 red bell peppers, chopped

Directions:
Put the chicken in a baking dish, add onion, garlic, salt, pepper, mushrooms, oil, and bell peppers. Mix briefly and bake in the oven at 425°F for 25minutes. Enjoy!

NUTRITION: Calories 285 Total Fat 11g Carbs 13g Protein 16g Fiber 1g

Lettuce Wraps with Smoked Trout

Prep Time: 10 minutes **Cooking Time:** 35 minutes **Servings:** 2

Ingredients:
1/2 unpeeled English hothouse cucumber (don't remove seeds) 1/4 cp thinly sliced shallots
1/4 cp thinly sliced jalapeño chiles with seeds (preferably red; about 2
large)
2 5oz packages skinless smoked trout fillets, broken into bitesize pieces (upto 2 cups)
2 tblpoons fresh lime juice or unseasoned rice vinegar 1 tbspoon sugar

1 tbspoon fish sauce (such as nam pla or nuoc nam) 2 medium carrots, peeled
1 cp diced grape tomatoes
1/3 cp Asian sweet chili sauce
1/4 cp finely chopped lightly salted dryroasted peanuts 1/2 cup whole fresh mint leaves
1/2 cup small whole fresh basil leaves
16 small to medium inner leaves of romaine lettuce (from about 2 hearts of romaine)

Directions:

Rasp carrots and cucumber lengthwise into ribbons using vegetable peeler. Cut ribbons into sections of 3 inches, then cut sections into strips of matchstick length. Set in a big bowl. Add jalapeños, sugar, shallots, lime juice, and fish sauce and marinate at room temperature for 30 minutes.

Add bits of trout and tomatoes to the mixture of vegetables and blend together. Transfer the mixture of trout and vegetables to the large strainer and drain the liquid. Return the mixture of trout and vegetable to the same bowl; add mint and basil and mix.

Arrange the leaves of lettuce on the large plate. Divide the lettuce leaves in the salad of the broccoli. Sprinkle each salad with sweet chili sauce and sprinkle with peanuts.

NUTRITION: Calories: 423Carbohydrates 60 gFat: 12 g Protein: 33g Saturated Fat: 2 g Sodium 1245 mg

Lemongrass and Ginger Mackerel

Prep Time: 10 minutes **Cooking Time**: 25 minutes **Servings**: 4

Ingredients:
4 mackerel fillets, skinless and boneless
2 tablespoons olive oil
1 tablespoon ginger, grated
2 lemongrass sticks, chopped
2 red chilies, chopped
Juice of 1 lime
A handful parsley, chopped

Directions:

In a roasting pan, combine the mackerel with the oil, ginger and the other ingredients, toss and bake at 390 degrees F for 25 minutes.
Divide everything between plates and serve.

NUTRITION: Calories: 251Fat: 3Fiber: 4Carbs: 14

Brown Rice and Shitake Miso Soup with Scallions

Servings: 4 Cooking Time: 45 Minutes

Ingredients:
2 tablespoons sesame oil
1 cup thinly sliced shiitake mushroom caps
1 garlic clove, minced
1 (1½inch) piece fresh ginger, peeled and sliced
1 cup mediumgrain brown rice

½ teaspoon salt
1 tablespoon white miso
2 scallions, thinly sliced
2 tablespoons finely chopped fresh cilantro

Directions:
Heatup the oil over mediumhigh heat in a large pot.
Add the mushrooms, garlic, and ginger and sauté until the mushrooms begin to soften about 5 minutes.
Put the rice and stir to coat with the oil evenly. Add 2 cups of water and salt and boil.
Simmer within 30 to 40 minutes. Use a little of the soup broth to soften the miso, then stir it into the pot until well blended.
Mix in the scallions plus cilantro, then serve.

NUTRITION: Calories 265 Total Fat: 8g Total Carbohydrates: 43g Sugar: 2g Fiber: 3g Protein: 5g Sodium: 456mg

Capellini Soup With Tofu And Shrimp

Servings: 8 **Cooking Time**: 20 Mins

Ingredients:
4 cups of bok choy, sliced
1/4pound shrimp, peeled, deveined
1 block firm tofu, sliced into squares
1 can sliced water chestnuts, drained
1 bunch scallions, sliced
2 cups reducedsodium chicken broth
2 teaspoons soy sauce, reducedsodium
2 cups capellini
2 teaspoons of sesame oil
Freshly ground white pepper
1 teaspoon of rice wine vinegar

Directions:
Pour the broth in a saucepan over mediumhigh heat. Bring to a boil. Add the shrimp, bok choy, oil, and sauce. Allow to boil and turn the heat to low. Simmer for 5 minutes.
Add the water chestnuts, pepper, vinegar, tofu, capellini, and scallions. Cook for 5 minutes or until the capellini is barely tender. Serve while hot.

NUTRITION: Calories 205 carbs: 20g fat: 9g protein: 9g

Chicken and Brussels sprouts

Prep Time: 10 minutes **Cooking Time**: 10 minutes **Servings**: 4

Ingredients:
1 cored, peeled and chopped apple
1 chopped yellow onion
1 tbsp. organic olive oil
3 c. shredded Brussels sprouts
1 lb. ground chicken meat

Black pepper

Directions:
Heat up a pan while using oil over mediumhigh heat, add chicken, stir and brown for 5 minutes.
Add Brussels sprouts, onion, black pepper and apple, stir, cook for 10
minutes, divide into bowls and serve.
1. Enjoy!

NUTRITION: Calories: 200Fat: 8 g Carbs: 13 g Protein: 9 g Sugars: 3 g Sodium: 194 mg

Bean Shawarma Salad

Servings: 2 **Cooking Time**: 20 Minutes

Ingredients:
For Preparing Salad
20 Pita chips
5ounces Spring lettuce
10 Cherry tomatoes
¾ Cup fresh parsley
¼ Cup red onion (chop)
For Chickpeas
1tablespoon Olive oil
1 Headingtablespoon cumin and turmeric
½ Headingtablespoon paprika and coriander powder
1 Pinch black pepper
½ Scant Kosher salt
¼tablespoon Ginger and cinnamon powder For Preparing Dressing
3 Garlic Cloves
1tablespoon Dried drill
1tablespoon Lime juice Water
½ Cup hummus

Directions:
Place a rack in the already preheated oven (204C). Mix chickpeas with all spices and herbs.
Place a thin layer of chickpeas on the baking sheet and bake it almost for 20
minutes. Bake it until the beans are golden brown.
For preparing the dressing, mix all ingredients in a whisking bowl and blend it.
Add water gradually for appropriate smoothness.
Mix all herbs and spices for preparing salad.
For serving, add pita chips and beans in the salad and drizzle some dressing over it.

NUTRITION: Calories 173 Carbs: 8g Fat: 6g Protein: 19g

Cod and Quinoa Mix

Prep Time: 10 minutes **Cooking Time**: 25 minutes **Servings**: 4

Ingredients
3 scallions, chopped
2 cups chicken stock

1 pound cod fillets, boneless and cubed
1 cup black quinoa
2 tablespoons olive oil
2 celery stalks, chopped
A pinch of salt and black pepper
1 tablespoon coriander, chopped

Directions:

Heat up a pan with the oil over mediumhigh heat, add the scallions and the celery and sauté for 5 minutes.
Add the fish and cook for 5 minutes more.
Add the rest of the ingredients, toss, cook over medium heat for 15 minutes more, divide everything between plates and serve.
NUTRITION: Calories: 261Fat: 4Fiber: 6Carbs: 14Protein: 7

Jicama Black Bean Salad

Prep Time: 10 minutes.　**Cook time**: 50 minutes.　**Serves**: 4

Ingredients:
1 cup mediumor longgrain brown rice
5 tablespoons extravirgin olive oil
2 teaspoons salt
1 (15ounce) can black beans, drained and rinsed 1 small jicama, peeled and cut into ¼inch dice ¼ cup chopped fresh cilantro
¼ cup lime juice, freshly squeezed
2 scallions, both white and green parts, sliced 1 small jalapeño pepper, seeded and minced
¼ teaspoon black pepper, freshly ground

Directions:
In a suitable pot, combine the rice, 2 cups of water, 1 tablespoon of oil, and 1
teaspoon of salt. Bring to a boil, Reduce its heat to a simmer, cover, and cook until the rice is tender, 40 to 45 minutes. Remove from the heat, let cool to room temperature, and fluff with a fork.
Add the beans, jicama, cilantro, lime juice, scallions, jalapeño pepper, remaining 4 tablespoons of oil, remaining 1 teaspoon of salt, and the pepper, and mix well. Serve at room temperature, or chill for several hours to serve cold.

NUTRITION: Calories 384; Fat 19g; Sodium 782mg; Carbs 57g; Fiber 14g; Sugars 7g; Protein 12g

Cherrybalsamic Chicken Breasts

Servings: 4 **Cooking Time**: 40 Minutes

Ingredients:
2 tbsp parsley, chopped
4 chicken breasts
2 scallions, sliced
2 tbsp coconut oil
¾ cup chicken broth
1 tbsp balsamic vinegar
½ cup dried cherries

Sea salt and pepper to taste

Directions:
Preheat your oven to 375ºF. Melt the coconut oil in a large skillet over medium heat. Season the chicken with salt and pepper. Place the chicken in the pan and brown it on both sides, 3 minutes per side. Add the scallions, chicken broth, balsamic vinegar, and dried cherries.
Cover with an ovenproof lid or aluminum foil and place the pan in the preheated oven. Bake for 20 minutes, or until the chicken is cooked through. Top with parsley.

NUTRITION: Per Serving: Calories: 380;Fat: 15g;Protein: 42g;Carbs: 17g.

Creamy Turkey With Mushrooms

Servings: 4 **Cooking Time**: 40 Minutes

Ingredients:
1 ½ lb turkey breasts, boneless and skinless 6 oz white button mushrooms, sliced
3 tbsp chopped shallots
½ tsp dried thyme
½ cup dry white wine
1 cup chicken stock
1 garlic clove, minced
2 tbsp olive oil
3 tbsp coconut cream
1 ½ tbsp arrowroot
Sea salt and pepper to taste

Directions:
Tie the turkey breast with a kitchen string horizontally, leaving approximately 2 inches apart. Season with salt and pepper. Heat half of the olive oil in your Instant Pot on "Sauté". Add the turkey and brown it for 3 minutes on each side. Transfer to a plate. Add the remaining oil, followed by the shallots, thyme, garlic, and mushrooms and cook for 5 minutes or until translucent. Add white wine and scrape up the brown bits from the bottom.
When the alcohol evaporates, return the turkey to the pot. Add the broth. Close the lid and cook for 20 minutes on "Manual". Combine the coconut cream and arrowroot in a bowl. Stir in the pot. Bring the sauce to a boil, then turn the cooker off. Slice the turkey in half and serve topped with the creamy mushroom sauce.

NUTRITION: Calories: 192;Fat: 5g;Protein: 15g;Carbs: 12g.

Shirataki Pasta with Avocado and Cream

Prep Time: 10minutes   **Total time**: 16   **Yield**: 2servings

Ingredients:
½ packet cooked
½ avocado
shirataki noodles
½ tsp. black pepper,
½ tsp. salt cracked
½ tsp. basil, dried

1/8 c. cream, heavy

Directions:
In a medium pot, add water until half full. Set over medium heat and allow to boil. Add in noodles and let cook for about 2minutes. Drain noodles and place them aside. Add avocado to a bowl and mash using a fork. Set in a blender alongside the other ingredients. Process well to get a smooth consistency. Set your heat to medium. Add noodles and avocado, mix in a frying pan and cook over heat for 2minutes. Serve.

NUTRITION: Calories 131 Total Fat 16g Total Carbs 9g Protein 2g Sugar 0.3g

Energy Bites

Prep time: 20 minutes **Cook time:** 0 minutes **Servings:** 24

Ingredients:
½ cup sunflower seeds
¼ cup pumpkin seeds
20 medium whole dates, pitted and chopped
¾ cup shredded coconut
½ cup cacao powder
2 tablespoons coconut oil
⅛ teaspoon salt
1 ½ tablespoons water

Directions:
Put seeds in a food processor and pulse until they are chopped (but not super fine like a powder).
Add dates, ½ cup shredded coconut, ¼ cup cacao, oil, salt, and water and process until ingredients are well mixed and mixture looks uniform.
Using a tablespoon, spoon out mixture and roll into balls.
Put the remaining ¼ cup shredded coconut and ¼ cup cacao on two separate flat plates. Coat balls with cacao or coconut by rolling half of balls in one, and half in the other. Place completed balls on a parchment paper–lined baking sheet.
Refrigerate at least 30 minutes (or up to overnight) until they harden. They will keep in refrigerator in an airtight container or plastic bag up to 2 weeks.

NUTRITION: Calories 56; Fat 3.51g; Sodium 25mg; Carbs 6.53g; Fiber 3g; Sugars 4.07g; Protein 1.5g

Banana Pops

Prep time: 15 minutes **Cook time:** 0 minutes **Servings:** 4

Ingredients:
¼ cup dark chocolate chips (cacao or higher) 2 large ripe bananas
4 popsicle sticks
½ cup plain, whole milk Greek yogurt
½ cup antiinflammatory granola, crushed into small chunks Prepare a baking sheet with parchment paper. Be sure tray will fit in a freezer.
Fill a medium saucepan ⅓ of the way with water. Place a suitable bowl on top of it. It should fit securely, but bottom of bowl should not touch bottom of pot. Place chocolate in bowl and melt, while stirring occasionally.
Peel bananas and cut them in half crosswise. Insert sticks into cut ends of bananas.

Place yogurt in a small shallow bowl.

Place granola on a flat plate.

To assemble, dip and roll banana in yogurt. Spread with back of a spoon or pastry brush to make sure it is well coated. Then roll banana in granola until it is evenly coated. Use your fingers to gently help granola stick.

Place banana pops on sheet and drizzle melted chocolate evenly over them.

Place tray in freezer at least 2 hours or up to overnight to firm up toppings.

Serve.

NUTRITION: Calories 179; Fat 11.9g; Sodium 30mg; Carbs 41.9g; Fiber 4.3g; Sugars 23.5g; Protein 7.9g

AlmondOrange Torte

Prep time: 45 minutes **Cook time:** 1 hr. 30 minutes **Servings:** 16

Ingredients:

3 large oranges

2 bay leaves

1 cinnamon stick

¾ cup sucanat

6 large eggs

½ teaspoon baking powder

3 ½ cups almond meal

1 cup hazelnut meal

¾ cup dark chocolate chips (cacao or higher) At 350 degrees F, preheat your oven grease and flour a 9" × 13" pan.

Directions:

In a medium pot, combine oranges, bay leaves, and cinnamon and cover with water. Bring to a boil and simmer over low heat 45 minutes until oranges are easily pierced with a fork. Cut them in quarters and let cool. Take out seeds and blend in a food processor until mash is chunky but even.

In a suitable bowl, combine orange purée, sucanat, eggs, baking powder, and nut meals. Mix well, then fold in chocolate chips.

Pour batter into prepared cake pan. Bake the food for 40–45 minutes.

Let cool at least 30 minutes before serving.

NUTRITION: Calories 220; Fat 16.6g; Sodium 36mg; Carbs 13.4g; Fiber 3.9g; Sugars 7.6g; Protein 8.2g

Peach Cobbler

Prep time: 10 minutes **Cook time:** 20 minutes **Servings:** 8

Ingredients:

1 teaspoon coconut oil plus ¼ cup, melted

2 cups sliced fresh nectarines

2 cups sliced fresh peaches

2 tablespoons lemon juice

¾ cup almond flour

¼ cup coconut sugar

¾ cup rolled oats

1 teaspoon ground cinnamon

½ teaspoon vanilla extract
Sea salt, to taste
Filtered water, for mixing

Directions:
At 425 degrees F, preheat your oven. Grease a baking sheet with 1 teaspoon of coconut oil.
Combine the nectarines, peaches, and lemon juice in the sheet. Stir to mix well. Set aside.
Put the almond flour, coconut sugar, oats, cinnamon, vanilla, salt, and remaining coconut oil in a food processor. Pulse until a dry dough forms.
Add a tablespoon of water if the dough is too dry.
Transfer the dough in a suitable bowl, then break the dough into chunks with your hands. Top the fruit in the baking sheet with the dough chunks.
Set the baking sheet in the preheated oven and bake for almost 20 minutes or until golden brown. Serve warm.

NUTRITION: Calories 137; Fat 6.3g; Sodium 36mg; Carbs 16.9g; Fiber 3.2g; Sugars 8.4g; Protein 4g

Applecinnamon Compote
Servings: 4 **Cooking Time**: 25 Minutes

Ingredients:
6 peeled apples, chopped
1 tsp fresh lemon juice
¼ cup orange juice
¼ cup honey
1 tsp ground cinnamon
A pinch of sea salt

Directions:
1. Place the apples, orange juice, lemon juice, honey, cinnamon, and salt in a pot over medium heat and simmer for 10 minutes until the apples are tender. Let cool completely before serving.

NUTRITION: Calories: 250;Fat: 1g;Protein: 8g;Carbs: 67g.

Delectable Honeyed Apple Cinnamon Compote
Servings: 4 **Cooking Time**: 10 Minutes

Ingredients:
6 apples, peeled, cored, and chopped
¼ cup apple juice
¼ cup honey
1 teaspoon cinnamon, ground
pinch sea salt

Directions:
1. Combine the apples, apple juice, honey, cinnamon, and salt in a large pot over mediumhigh heat. Simmer for 10 minutes while stirring occasionally until the apples are quite chunky and saucy.

NUTRITION: Calories: 247 ;Protein: 1g ;Carbs: 66g .

Crème Caramel Coconut Flan

Servings: 4 **Cooking Time:** 30 Minutes

Ingredients:

2 eggs
7 oz coconut milk
½ cups coconut milk
½ tsp vanilla
1 cup brown sugar

Directions:

1. Place a pan with a heavy bottom in your Instant Pot. Place the sugar in the pan. Cook until a caramel is formed. Divide the caramel between 4
small ramekins. Pour 1 cup of water into the pressure cooker and lower the trivet. Beat the rest of the ingredients together and divide them between the ramekins. Cover them with aluminum foil and place in the pot. Close the lid and cook for 5 minutes on "Manual". Release the pressure naturally for 10 minutes. Serve and enjoy!

NUTRITION: Calories: 110;Fat: 3g;Protein: 3g;Carbs: 16g.

Raisin Oatmeal Biscuits

Servings: 6 **Cooking Time:** 20 Minutes

Ingredients:

½ cup almond butter
1 cup date sugar
¼ cup pineapple juice
1 cup wholegrain flour
1 tsp baking powder
½ tsp salt
1 tsp vanilla extract
1 cup oldfashioned oats
½ cup dark chocolate chips
½ cup raisins

Directions:

1. Preheat your oven to 370ºF. Beat the almond butter and date sugar in a bowl until creamy and fluffy. Pour in the juice and blend. Mix in flour, baking powder, salt, and vanilla. Stir in oats, chocolate chips, and raisins. Spread the dough on a baking sheet and bake for 15 minutes.
Let completely cool on a rack. Serve and enjoy!

NUTRITION: Calories: 385;Fat: 17g;Protein: 6g;Carbs: 60g.

Raspberry and Chard Smoothie

Prep time: 5 minutes **Cooking time:** 0 minute **Servings:** 2

Chard and raspberry might not be your favorites, but they are rich in antioxidants and curb inflammation.

Ingredients:

2 C. coconut water
2 C. Swiss chards
2 key limes, juiced
2 C. fresh whole raspberries

Directions:

Whizz all the ingredients on high.
Pour into a cup and enjoy.

NUTRITION: Calories: 133.7 kcal Carbohydrates: 31.02 g Fat: 1.47 g Fiber: 12.8 g Protein: 4.2 g

Apple, Berries, and Kale Smoothie

Prep time: 5 minutes **Cooking time:** 0 minute **Servings:** 2

Say goodbye to digestive issues, joint problems and get your daily vitamin C dose in a gulp.

Ingredients:

1 C. spring water
1 C. berries, mixed – blueberries are good
2 C. kale leaves, fresh
1 large apple, cored

Directions:

Whizz all the ingredients on high.
Pour into a cup and enjoy.

NUTRITION: Calories: 119.27 kcal Carbohydrates: 28.55 g Fat: 0.96 g Fiber: 5.3 g Protein: 3.5 g

Orange Banana Alkaline Smoothie

Prep time: 10 minutes **Cooking time:** 0 minutes **Servings:** 2

Ingredients:

½ C. coconut water
1 C. water
2 mediumsize bananas
4 oranges, peeled
¼ tsp. bromide plus powder
2 tsp. lightcolored agave syrup

Directions:

Mash the banana and pour all ingredients into a blender. Blend in 2030 second increments until the mixture is smooth.
Dilute with water to your desired thickness.
Serve in a cup and add some ice cubes or place in a refrigerator.

NUTRITION: Calories: 223.99 kcal Protein: 3.45 g Sugar: 37.84 g Fiber:1.8.14 g

Easy Pork Chops

Prep time: 10 minutes **Cooking Time:**20 or so minutes **Servings:** 4

Ingredients:
4 pork chops, boneless
1 tablespoon extravirgin olive oil
1 cup chicken stock, lowsodium
A pinch of black pepper
1 teaspoon sweet paprika

Directions:
1. Heat up a pan while using the oil over mediumhigh heat, add pork chops, brown them for 5 minutes on either sides, add paprika, black pepper and stock, toss, cook for fifteen minutes more, divide between plates and serve by using a side salad.
2. Enjoy!

NUTRITION: Calories: 272Fat: 4Fiber: 8Carbs: 14Protein: 17

Cod Soup

Prep time: 10 minutes **Cooking Time:** 25 minutes **Servings:** 4

Ingredients:
1 yellow onion, chopped
12 cups lowsodium fish stock
1 pound carrots, sliced
1 tablespoon extravirgin organic olive oil
Black pepper on the taste
2 tablespoons ginger, minced
1 cup water
1 pound cod, skinless, boneless and cut into medium chunks

Directions:
1. Heat up a pot using the oil over mediumhigh heat, add onion, stir and cook for 4 minutes.
2. Add water, stock, ginger and carrots, stir and cook for 10 mins more.
3. Blend soup employing an immersion blender, add the fish and pepper, stir, cook for 10 mins more, ladle into bowls and serve.
4. Enjoy!

NUTRITION: Calories: 261Fat: 6Fiber: 2Carbs: 11Protein: 9

Easy Beef Stew

Prep time: 10 mins **Cooking Time:** 60 minutes and twenty or so minutes **Servings: 6**

Ingredients:
2 and ½ pounds beef brisket
Fat: removed
2 bay leaves

4 cups lowsodium beef stock
4 carrots, chopped
3 garlic cloves, chopped
1 green cabbage head, shredded
Black pepper towards the taste

Directions

1. Put the beef brisket in a pot, add stock, pepper, garlic and bay leaves, provide your simmer over medium heat and cook for an hour.
2. Add carrots and cabbage, stir, cook for a halfhour more, divide into bowls and serve for lunch.

NUTRITION: Calories: 271Fat: 8Fiber: 3Carbs: 16Protein: 9

Sweet Potato Soup

Prep time: 10 mins **Cooking Time:** 1 hour or so and 40 minutes **Servings: 6**

Ingredients:
4 big sweet potatoes
28 ounces veggie stock
A pinch of black pepper
¼ teaspoon nutmeg, ground
1/3 cup lowsodium heavy cream

Directions:

1. Arrange the sweet potatoes around the lined baking sheet, bake them at 350 degrees F for 60 minutes and thirty minutes, cool them down, peel, roughly chop them and put them inside the pot.
2. Add stock, nutmeg, cream and pepper, pulse effectively utilizing an immersion blender, heat the soup over medium heat, cook for 10
minutes, ladle into bowls and serve.
NUTRITION: Calories: 235Fat: 4Fiber: 5Carbs: 16Protein: 8

Classic Vegetable Broth

Prep time: 15 minutes or fewer **Cooking Time:** 6 to 8 hours on low **Servings: 12 cups**
Ingredients:
Extravirgin olive oil, for coating the slow cooker 6 cups veggie scraps (peels and pieces of carrots, celery, onions, garlic) 12 cups filtered water
½ medium onion, roughly chopped
2 garlic cloves, roughly chopped
1 parsley sprig
¾ teaspoon sea salt
½ teaspoon dried oregano
½ teaspoon dried basil leaves
2 bay leaves

Directions:

1. Coat the slow cooker with a thin layer of olive oil.

2. In the slow cooker, combine the veggie scraps, water, onion, garlic, parsley, salt, oregano, basil, and bay leaves.
3. Cover the cooker and set to low. Cook for 6 to 8 hours.
4. Pour the broth through a finemesh sieve set over a large bowl, discarding the veggie scraps. Refrigerate the broth in airtight containers for up to 5 days, or freeze for up to 3 months.

NUTRITION: Calories: 24Fat: 0gTotal Carbs: 5gSugar: 2gFiber: 1g Protein: 1g Sodium: 202mg

Simple Spaghetti Squash

Prep time: 15 minutes or fewer, plus 15 minutes to cool **Cooking Time:** 8 hours
Servings: 46

Ingredients:
1 spaghetti squash, washed well
2 cups water

Directions:
1. Using a fork, poke 10 to 15 holes all around the outside of the spaghetti squash. Put the squash and the water in your slow cooker.
2. Cover the cooker and set to low. Cook for 8 hours.
3. Transfer the squash from the slow cooker to a cutting board. Let sit for 15 minutes to cool.
4. Halve the squash lengthwise. Using a spoon, scrape the seeds out of the center of the squash. Then, using a fork, scrape at the flesh until it shreds into a spaghettilike texture. Serve warm.

NUTRITION: Calories: 60Total Fat: 0gTotal Carbs: 15gSugar: 0g Protein: 0g Sodium: 42mg

Stuffed Sweet Potatoes

Prep time: 15 minutes or fewer **Cooking Time:** 6 to 7 hours on low **Servings:** 4
Ingredients:
4 medium sweet potatoes
1 cup Hatch Chile "Refried" Beans

4 tablespoons chopped scallions (both white and green parts) 1 avocado, peeled, pitted, and quartered
Directions:
1. Wash the sweet potatoes, but do not dry them. The water left on the skins from washing is the only moisture needed for cooking. Put the damp sweet potatoes in your slow cooker.
2. Cover the cooker and set to low. Cook for 6 to 7 hours. A fork should easily poke through when they are done.
3. Carefully remove the hot sweet potatoes from the slow cooker. Slice each one lengthwise about halfway through. Mash the revealed flesh with a fork, and fill the opening with ¼ cup of beans. Top each with 1
tablespoon of scallions and a quarter of the avocado and serve.

NUTRITION: Calories: 237Total Fat: 8gTotal Carbs: 38gSugar: 7gFiber: 10g Protein: 6g Sodium: 315mg

JamPacked Peppers

Prep time: 15 minutes or fewer **Cooking Time**: 4 to 5 hours on low **Servings: 4**

Ingredients:

1 tablespoon avocado oil

4 bell peppers, any color, washed, tops cut off, and seeded ½ cup water

2 cups Spanish Rice

1 (15ounce) can black beans, rinsed and drained well

Directions:

1. Coat the bottom of the slow cooker with the avocado oil.

2. Place the peppers, upright, in the cooker. Add the water to the bottom of the slow cooker, around the outside of the peppers.

3. In a large bowl, stir together the rice and black beans. Stuff each pepper with onequarter of the mixture.

4. Cover the cooker and set to low. Cook for 4 to 5 hours and serve.

NUTRITION: Calories: 340Total Fat: 9gTotal Carbs: 58gSugar: 3gFiber: 7g Protein: 9g Sodium: 687mg

Vegan "Frittata"

Prep Time: 15 minutes **Cooking Time**: 20 minutes **Servings**: 6

Ingredients:

1½ cups garbanzo bean flour

1 teaspoon salt

1 teaspoon ground turmeric

½ teaspoon ground cumin

1 teaspoon chopped fresh sage

1½ cups water

2 tablespoons extravirgin olive oil

1 zucchini, sliced

2 scallions, sliced

Directions:

Preheat the oven to 350°F.

In a medium bowl, whisk together the garbanzo bean flour, salt, turmeric, cumin, and sage.

Slowly add the water, stirring constantly to prevent the batter from getting lumpy. Set aside.

In an ovensafe skillet, heat the oil over high heat. Sauté the zucchini until softened, 2 to 3 minutes. Stir in the scallions, then spoon the batter over the vegetables.

Place the skillet in the oven and bake until firm when jiggled slightly, 20 to 25 minutes.

Serve warm or at room temperature.

NUTRITION: Calories: 140Total Fat: 6gTotal Carbohydrates: 15gSugar: 3gFiber: 3g Protein: 6g Sodium: 410mg

Beets Gazpacho

Prep Time: 10minutes   **Total time**: 20minutes   **Yield**: 4servings

Ingredients:

1× 20oz. Can Great Northern Beans,
¼ tsp. Kosher Salt rinsed and drained
1 tbsp. ExtraVirgin Olive Oil
½ tsp. Garlic, fresh and minced
1× 6oz. pouch Pink Salmon flaked
2 tbsp. Lemon juice, freshly squeezed
4 Green Onions, sliced thinly
½ tsp. Ground Black Pepper
½ tsp. Lemon rind grated
¼ c. Flatleaf Parsley, fresh and chopped

Directions:

First, place lemon rind, olive oil, lemon juice, black pepper, and garlic in a mediumsized mixing bowl and mix them with a whisker. Combine beans, onions, salmon, and parsley in another mediumsized bowl and toss them well. Then, spoon in the lemon juice dressing over the bean's mixture. Mix well ùntil the dressing coats the beans mixture. Serve and enjoy.

NUTRITION: Calories 131, Proteins: 9g Carbohydrates: 18g Fat: 5g

Baked Butternut Squash Rigatoni

Prep Time: 10minutes   **Total time**: 1hour 40minutes   **Yield**: 4servings

Ingredients:

1 enormous
3 clove garlic butternut squash
2 tbsp. olive oil
1 lb. rigatoni
1/2 c. substantial
3 c. destroyed cream fontina
2 tbsp. slashed crisp
1 tbsp. salt sage
1 tsp. naturally,
1 c. panko ground pepper breadcrumbs

Directions:

Preheat broiler to 425 degrees F. In the meantime, in a huge bowl, hurl squash, garlic, and olive oil to cover. Spot on a huge rimmed preparing sheet and dish until delicate, around 60minutes. Set your container on a wire rack
to allow for cooling, around 10minutes. Decrease stove to 350 degrees F. In the meantime, heat a huge pot of salted water to the point of boiling and cook rigatoni as per bundle bearings. Channel and put in a safe spot. Utilizing a blender or nourishment processor, purée held squash with overwhelming cream until smooth. In a huge bowl, hurl squash puree withheld rigatoni, 2
cups fontina, savvy, salt, and pepper. Brush base and sides of a 9by 13inch preparing dish with olive oil. Move rigatonisquash blend to a dish.

In a little bowl, consolidate the remaining fontina and panko. Sprinkle over pasta and heat until brilliant darker, 20 to 25minutes.

NUTRITION: 654kcal , Protein: 343 g, Fat: 492 g, Carbohydrates: 217 g

Chicken Lettuce Wraps

Prep Time: 20 minutes   **Cook time**: 0 minutes   **Serves** 4

Ingredients:
2 heads butter lettuce, 8 lettuce cups total
1 pound (454 g) grilled boneless skinon chicken breast, cut into ½inch cubes
1 cup shredded carrots
½ cup thinly sliced radishes
2 scallions, sliced thinly
2 tablespoons chopped fresh cilantro
½ cup toasted sesame oil
3 tablespoons freshly squeezed lime juice
1 tablespoon coconut aminos
1 garlic clove
1 thin slice fresh ginger
1 teaspoon lime zest
1 tablespoon sesame seeds, divided

Directions:
 Place the lettuce cups on a serving platter. Evenly divide the chicken, carrots, radishes, scallions, and cilantro among the lettuce cups. In a blender or food processor, combine the sesame oil, lime juice, coconut aminos, garlic, ginger, and lime zest. Blend until smooth. Drizzle the chicken and vegetables with the dressing and sprinkle each with sesame seeds.

NUTRITION: Calories: 342   fat: 30g   protein: 7g   carbs: 13g   fiber: 3g   sugar: 4g   sodium: 40mg

Dinner

New England Clam Chowder

Prep Time: 15 minutes.   **Cook time**: 8 minutes.   **Serves**: 4

Ingredients:
3 (5ounce) cans clams, drained, juice reserved, and chopped ½ cup water
2 tablespoons ghee
2 garlic cloves, minced
2 celery stalks, chopped
1 yellow onion, diced
1 teaspoon sea salt
¼ teaspoon black pepper, freshly ground
1½ pounds Yukon gold potatoes, diced
¼ teaspoon dried thyme
1 ⅓ cups coconut milk

Directions:

In a glass measuring cup, combine the reserved clam juice and water, adding more water as needed to equal 2 cups total. Set aside.

Select sauté on the instant pot and let the pot preheat.

Set the ghee in the pot to melt and add the garlic, celery, onion, salt, and pepper. Cook for almost 3 minutes.

Add the clam juicewater mixture and the potatoes and stir to combine. Turn off the heat. Lock the lid.

Select the pressure cook and cook at high pressure for almost 5 minutes.

When cooked, use a quick release.

Remove the lid and stir in the clams, thyme, and coconut milk. Cook for almost 2 minutes with the residual heat from the pot to warm, then serve.

NUTRITION: Calories 414; Fat 19g; Sodium 912mg; Carbs 55g; Fiber 5g; Sugars 4g; Protein 3g

Aromatic Turkey With Mushrooms

Servings: 4 **Cooking Time**: 4 Hours 15 Minutes

Ingredients:

2 cups button mushrooms, sliced
2 turkey thighs
1 red bell pepper, sliced
1 large onion, sliced
1 garlic clove, sliced
1 tbsp extravirgin olive oil
1 rosemary sprig
Sea salt and pepper to taste
2 cups chicken broth
½ cup dry red wine

Directions:

Grease your slow cooker with olive oil. Add the turkey thighs, bell pepper, mushrooms, onion, garlic, rosemary sprig, salt, and pepper.

Pour in the chicken broth and wine. Cover and cook on "High" for 4

hours. Remove and discard the rosemary sprig. Use a slotted spoon to transfer the thighs to a plate and allow them to cool for several minutes for easier handling. Cut the meat from the bones, stir the meat into the mushrooms, and serve.

NUTRITION: Per Serving: Calories: 275;Fat: 9g;Protein: 42g;Carbs: 3g.

Crispy Chicken Tenderloin

Servings: 4 **Cooking Time:** 15 Minutes

Ingredients:

1 egg, beaten 8 chicken tenderloin
2 tablespoons avocado oil
½ cup breadcrumbs

Directions:
Preheat your air fryer to 350 degrees F.
Dip chicken in egg.
Mix oil and breadcrumbs.
Coat chicken with this mixture.
Add to the air fryer basket.
Cook for 15 minutes.

Lemony Salmon

Prep Time: 10 minutes. **Cooking time**: **1 hour. Servings: 2**

Ingredients:
1 big salmon fillet, halved
1 Teaspoon olive oil
A pinch of salt and black pepper

For the relish:
1 tablespoon lemon juice
1 shallot, chopped
1 Meyer lemon, cut in wedges, and then thinly sliced 1 Tablespoon parsley, chopped
¼ cup olive oil

Directions:
 Arrange the salmon on a lined baking dish, drizzle 2 teaspoons of olive oil, season with sea salt and black pepper and rub the seasoning into the fish. Place in the oven at 370ºF and bake for 1 hour.
 In a bowl, mix shallot with the lemon juice, salt, and black pepper, stir and leave aside for 10 minutes. In another bowl, whisk together the marinated shallot with lemon slices, some salt, pepper, parsley, and ¼
cup oil. Cut salmon in chunks, divide between plates, top with lemon relish, and serve. Enjoy!

NUTRITION: Calories: 200 Fat**:** 8 g Fiber: 3 g Carbs: 6 g Protein: 10 g

Chicken Curry in Parchment

Servings: 4 **Cooking Time:** 30 Minutes

Ingredients:
3 large chickens, neck and heart reserved for Easy chicken Stock ¼ cup finely minced garlic
Sea salt
Freshly ground black pepper
Curry Vinaigrette Ingredients
3/4 cup coriander
1/4 cup parsley
½ tsp. cumin
½ tsp. curry powder
½ tsp. fennel seeds
1 pinch turmeric
4 small garlic cloves, peeled
1/2 cup extra virgin olive oil, room temperature 1 tsp. Vinegar Sea salt

Directions:

Bring the turkey to room temperature by letting it sit for an hour Combine the vinaigrette ingredients in a food processor Preheat your oven to 325 degrees and placed the rack on the lower third.

Rub the neck cavity with the vinaigrette, salt and pepper.

Stuff the chickens with the lemons

Divide and spread 6 tablespoons of vinaigrette over the top of the chicken as well and season with salt and pepper.

Spread the remaining vinaigrette on a 40 inch sheet of parchment paper.

Place the chicken on top with a short side facing up.

Wrap the chicken with a parchment paper and crimp the edges.

Place this on top of a 48 in sheet of parchment paper Rotate 90 degrees, fold the short parchment sides over the turkey and crimp the edges.

Place the chicken on a roasting pan.

Roast for 2 hours and 20 minutes or until the internal temp. of each chicken reaches 155 degrees F.

Take it out of the oven and remove the parchment paper.

Beef, Pork, and Lamb Thai Beef with Coconut Milk

Prep Time: 10 minutes   **Cook time**: 30 minutes   Serves 2

Ingredients:

2 tablespoons coconut oil

1 teaspoon crushed garlic

1 onion cut into wedges

8 ounces (227 g) round steak, cut into strips

2 cups cubed potatoes

1 lime

2 cups cubed Carrots

1 cup coconut milk

½cup beef stock

Black pepper to taste

Directions:

Heat the wok over a medium heat, and then add in the oil, garlic, and the onion, cooking for 1 minute. Put the beef into the wok and cook for 3

minutes. Add in the potatoes, Carrots into the wok and stirfry for 4

minutes. Add the coconut milk, beef stock, and black pepper and allow to simmer for 20 to 25 minutes or until beef is cooked through. Serve hot with your choice of greens and a wedge of lime to squeeze!

NUTRITION: Calories: 563 fat: 45g protein: 30g carbs: 15g fiber: 3g sugar: 4g sodium: 235mg

Berry Bliss Slow Cooker Pork

Prep Time: 10 minutes **Cook time**: 6 hours **Serves** 4

Ingredients:

4 thickcut boneless pork chops

1 teaspoon fine Himalayan salt

½ teaspoon ground black pepper

2 tablespoons avocado oil

2 cups raspberries or blackberries

½ cup bone broth
½ cup chopped red onions
¼ cup chopped fresh parsley
¼ cup red wine vinegar
1 teaspoon peeled and minced fresh ginger
Pinch of ground nutmeg
Dash of ground cinnamon
10 drops liquid stevia (optional)

Directions:
Heat a large skillet over medium heat, or heat an electric pressure cooker on sauté mode. Sprinkle the pork chops with the salt and pepper. When the skillet or pressure cooker is hot, pour in the oil and sear the chops for 3
minutes on each side. Place the seared pork chops in the slow cooker so they are all lying flat. Add the remaining ingredients. Cover and cook on low for 6 hours. Remove the lid from the slow cooker and use tongs to carefully remove the pork chops. Serve with the tender berries and sauce spooned on top of the chops. It's quite lovely. Store leftovers in an airtight container in the fridge for up to 4 days. Reheat in a covered skillet over medium heat for 5 to 10 minutes.

NUTRITION: Calories: 432   fat: 14g   protein: 44g   carbs: 32g   fiber: 5g   sugar: 26g   sodium: 545mg

Fake Mushroom Risotto

Servings: 4 **Cooking Time**: 30 Minutes

Ingredients:
1 ½ head cauliflower
2 cups sliced mushrooms
1 garlic clove, minced
1 tsp dried basil
1 carrot, grated
1 cup vegetable broth
1 tbsp olive oil
½ onion, diced

Directions:
Cut the cauliflower into pieces and place them in your food processor.
Process until really ground (cauliflower rice). You should have about 6 cups of cauliflower rice.
Heat the oil in your Instant Pot set to "Sauté". Sauté the carrots and onions for 3 minutes. Add the garlic and cook for one more minute.
Stir in all of the remaining ingredients. Seal lid and press "Manual"
function. Cook for 5 minutes. Do a quick pressure release. Serve.

NUTRITION: Calories: 120;Fat: 11g;Protein: 3g;Carbs: 14g.

Chicken with Fennel and Zucchini

Prep Time: 15 minutes   **Cook time**: 15 minutes   **Serves** 4

Ingredients:
2 tablespoons
extravirgin olive oil
4 boneless skinless chicken breasts, cut into strips 1 leek, white part only, sliced thinly
1 fennel bulb, sliced into ¼inch rounds
3 zucchini, sliced into ½inch rounds
½ cup chicken broth
1 teaspoon salt
½ teaspoon freshly ground black pepper
½ cup sliced green olives
2 tablespoons chopped fresh dill

Directions:
In a large pan over high heat, heat the olive oil. Add the chicken strips.
Brown them for 1 to 2 minutes, stirring constantly. Transfer the chicken and its juices to a plate or bowl and set aside. Add the leek, fennel, and zucchini to the pan. Sauté for 5 minutes. Return the chicken and juices to the pan. Pour in the broth. Add the salt and pepper. Cover the pan and simmer for 5 minutes. Remove the pan from the heat, and stir in the olives and dill.

NUTRITION: Calories: 418   fat: 20g   protein: 45g   carbs: 15g Fibre: 4g   sugar: 5g sodium: 1021mg

Rosemary Pork Chops

Whether you use fresh or dehydrated rosemary, the benefits are huge and this is delicious.

Prep Time: 30 minutes **Cooking time**: 35 minutes **Servings**: 4

Ingredients
4 pork loin chops, boneless
Salt and black pepper, to taste
4 garlic cloves, minced
1 tbsp. rosemary, chopped
1 tbsp. olive oil

Directions
Combine the pork chops with the rest of the ingredients in a roasting plan, toss, and bake at 425°F for 10 minutes.
Reduce the heat to 350°F and cook the chops for 25 minutes more.
Divide the chops between plates and serve with a side salad.

NUTRITION: Calories: 2678 kcal Fat: 103 g Fiber: 0.2 g Carbs: 26 g Protein: 356 g

Mushroom Risotto

Prep Time: 5 Minutes **Cooking Time**: 25 Minutes **Servings**: 4

Ingredients:
2 Tablespoons Olive Oil
1 Shallot, Large & Sliced Thin

10 Cremini Mushrooms, Sliced
½ Cup Red Wine, Dry
1 Cup Arborio Rice
1 ½ 2 Cups Vegetable Broth
½ Cup Parmesan Cheese, Grated
1 Tablespoon Parsley, Freshly Chopped
1 Teaspoon Sea Salt, Fine
Black Pepper to Taste

Directions:

Heat your oil in a skillet using high heat, and then add in your shallot. Cook for three to five minutes or until softened.
Add your mushrooms and red wine, simmering until the wine evaporates.
Add in your rice, cooking for three more minutes.
Add in a half a cup of your broth, cooking and stirring until it's been absorbed. Repeat until your risotto is tender, but it shouldn't be mushy. This should take roughly twenty minutes.
Remove from heat, sprinkling with parsley, parmesan, salt and pepper. Serve warm.

NUTRITION: Calories: 320Kcal Proteins: 10g Carbohydrates: 829g Fat: 11g

Slow Cooker Shawarma

Prep time: 10 minutes **Cook time:** 8 hours **Serves** 6

Ingredients:
1 tablespoon fine Himalayan salt
1 tablespoon ground black pepper
1 tablespoon ground cumin
1 teaspoon ground cardamom
½ teaspoon ground nutmeg
3 pounds (1.4 kg) boneless chuck short rib or shoulder ¼ cup coconut vinegar or red wine vinegar
3 tablespoons avocado oil
5 cloves garlic, peeled
1 large onion, quartered
1 lemon, quartered
1 navel orange, quartered

Directions:

1. In a small bowl, mix together the salt, pepper, cumin, cardamom, and nutmeg. Rub the spice mixture all over the meat. 2. Place the meat in a large bowl and drizzle the vinegar and oil all over it. Add the garlic, onion, and citrus. Toss to combine, squeezing some juice out of the fruit. Cover and set in the refrigerator to marinate overnight. 3. When you're ready to cook, put everything in the slow cooker, meat on the bottom, citrus and onion quarters on top. Cook on low for 8 hours. 4. Discard the large pieces of citrus. Use two forks to shred the beef. If you like crispy beef, you can spread it on a sheet pan and broil it for 5 minutes to get delicious crispy tips. Divide the shredded beef among five or six plates, spoon the delicious slow cooker sauce over the meat, and serve. 5. Store leftovers in an airtight container in the fridge for up to 5 days or in the freezer for up to 30 days. To thaw and reheat, place in a preheated 400ºF (205ºC) oven for 10 to 20 minutes.

NUTRITION: Calories: 496 fat: 28g protein: 54g carbs: 8g fiber: 2g sugar: 2g sodium: 600mg

Garlicky Lamb Stew

Prep time: 15 minutes **Cook time:** 15 minutes **Serves** 4

Ingredients:

1 pound (454 g) ground lamb
1 tablespoon extravirgin olive oil
1 onion, chopped
1 teaspoon dried oregano
½ teaspoon sea salt
¼ teaspoon freshly ground black pepper
1 (28 ounces / 794 g) can chopped tomatoes, drained 5 garlic cloves, minced

Directions:

1. In a large nonstick skillet over mediumhigh heat, cook the lamb for about 5 minutes, crumbling it with a wooden spoon until it browns. Drain the fat and remove the lamb to a dish. 2. Return the skillet to the heat, add the olive oil, and heat it until it shimmers. 3. Add the onion, oregano, salt, and pepper. Cook for 5 minutes, stirring, until the onions are soft. 4. Return the lamb to the skillet and stir in the tomatoes. Cook for 3 minutes, stirring occasionally, or until heated through. 5. Add the garlic. Cook for 30 seconds, stirring constantly.

NUTRITION: Calories: 295 fat: 12g protein: 34g carbs: 12g fiber: 3g sugar: 7g sodium: 332mg

Pork Sausage

Prep time: 10 minutes **Cook time:** 15 minutes **Makes** 10 patties

Ingredients:

2 pounds (907 g) ground pork
2 ribs celery, minced
4 cloves garlic, minced
2 teaspoons Dijon mustard
2 teaspoons fine Himalayan salt
1 teaspoon dried thyme leaves
1 teaspoon ground black pepper
¼ teaspoon ginger powder
¼ teaspoon ground cinnamon
Pinch of ground nutmeg

Directions:

1. Place all of the ingredients in a large bowl and mix thoroughly with your hands. 2. Heat a large castiron skillet over medium heat. While it heats, shape the pork mixture into patties, about ¼ cup per patty. 3. When the skillet is hot, place four or five patties in the pan, without crowding the pan. Cook the patties for 6 minutes per side, or until the internal temperature reaches 165ºF (74ºC). Repeat with the remaining patties. 4. This sausage stores well side by side in an airtight container in the refrigerator for up to 5 days or in the freezer for up to 30 days. To reheat, place in a preheated 350ºF (180ºC) oven for 8 to 10 minutes.

NUTRITION: Calories: 157 fat: 12g protein: 9g carbs: 2g fiber: 0g sugar: 0g sodium: 364mg

Yogurt with Dates

Prep time: 5 minutes. **Cook time:** 0 minutes. **Serves:** 4

Ingredients:
2 cups coconut yogurt, unsweetened
¼ cup chopped almonds
¼ cup chopped walnuts
2 pitted dates, chopped
½ teaspoon ground cinnamon

Directions:
In a suitable bowl, stir together the yogurt, almonds, walnuts, dates, and cinnamon. Serve immediately.

NUTRITION: Calories 161; Fat 10.7g; Sodium 25mg; Carbs 11.8g; Fiber 2g; Sugars 8.9g; Protein 6.3g

Bean Salsa

Prep time: 20 minutes. **Cook time:** 30 minutes. **Serves:** 6

Ingredients:
1 cup dried pinto beans, rinsed
3 cups vegetable broth
1 teaspoon sea salt
1 red onion, chopped
1 cup fresh cilantro, chopped
1 cup chopped tomatoes
1 avocado, peeled, halved, pitted, and diced 1 small jalapeño pepper, seeded and minced
1 cup frozen corn
Juice of 1 lime
Organic blue corn chips, for serving

Directions:
In the instant pot, combine the beans, broth, and salt. Lock the lid.
Presssure cook at high for almost 30 minutes.
While the beans cook, in a suitable bowl, stir together the red onion, cilantro, tomatoes, avocado, and jalapeño. Set aside.
When cooking is complete, use a natural release.
Remove the lid and stir in the frozen corn. Transfer the bean mixture to the bowl with the tomato and cilantro mixture, add the lime juice, and stir to combine well. Serve with the corn chips.

NUTRITION: Calories 235; Fat 8g; Sodium 707mg; Carbs 31.3g; Fiber 8.8g; Sugars 3.6g; Protein 11.3g

Toasted Nut Mix

Prep time: 5 minutes. **Cook time:** 6 minutes approximately. **Serves:** 6

Ingredients:
1 cup raw cashews

1 cup raw almonds
1 teaspoon ghee
¼ teaspoon curry powder
¼ teaspoon garlic powder
¼ teaspoon sea salt

Directions:
Layer a plate with a paper towel and set aside.
Select sauté on the instant pot and let the pot preheat.
In the pot, combine the cashews and almonds. Toast for almost 6 minutes, while stirring frequently to keep the nuts from burning, until they begin to brown lightly.
Add the ghee, curry powder, garlic powder, and salt, mixing well until the nuts are thoroughly coated.
Transfer the seasoned nuts to the prepared plate to cool. The cashews will be slightly chewy when warm.
Store in an airtight container in a cool dark cabinet for up to 5 days.

NUTRITION: Calories 172; Fat 14.4g; Sodium 61mg; Carbs 8.3g; Fiber 2g; Sugars 1.4g; Protein 5.2g

Brussels Sprouts with Walnuts

Prep time: 15 minutes. **Cook time:** 11 minutes. **Serves:** 4

Ingredients:
1½ pounds Brussels sprouts
¼ cup ghee
3 garlic cloves, minced
½ teaspoon sea salt
¼ teaspoon black pepper
1 cup vegetable broth
1 tablespoon Dijon mustard
½ cup raw walnuts, chopped

Directions:
Select sauté on the instant pot and let the pot preheat.
Set the brussels sprouts in the pot and add the ghee, garlic, salt, and pepper.
Cook for almost 6 minutes approximately.
Stir in the broth and mustard, mixing well to combine. Turn off heat. Lock the lid.
Pressure cook at high for almost 5 minutes.
When cooking is complete, use a quick release. Remove the lid.
Sprinkle the Brussels sprouts with the walnuts and serve.

NUTRITION: Calories 298; Fat 23.1g; Sodium 513mg; Carbs 18.3g; Fiber 7.7g; Sugars 4.1g; Protein 11.1g

Mixed Mushrooms with Herbs

Prep time: 15 minutes. **Cook time:** 6 minutes approximately. **Serves:** 4

Ingredients:
¼ cup ghee
3 garlic cloves, minced
1 cup cremini mushrooms, chopped

1 cup shiitake mushrooms, chopped
1 cup beech mushrooms, chopped
¼ cup vegetable broth
½ cup fresh parsley, chopped
1 teaspoon Italian seasoning
1 teaspoon sea salt
½ teaspoon black pepper

Directions:
Select sauté on the instant pot and let the pot preheat.
Set the ghee and garlic into the pot and cook until lightly browned.
Stir in the cremini, shiitake, and beech mushrooms, the broth, parsley, Italian seasoning, salt, and pepper until well coated. Turn off the heat. Lock the lid.
Select pressure cook and cook at high pressure for almost 1 minute.
When cooking is complete, use a quick release.
Remove the lid and serve.

NUTRITION: Calories 172; Fat 13.9g; Sodium 610mg; Carbs 14.7g; Fiber 5.2g; Sugars 1.8g; Protein 4.8g

Sweet Potato Mash
Prep time: 10 minutes. **Cook time:** 25 minutes. **Serves:** 4

Ingredients:
1 cup water
4 large (8 to 12ounce) sweet potatoes, pierced with a fork multiple times 1 teaspoon ghee
½ teaspoon sea salt, more for garnish
¼ teaspoon ground nutmeg
½ cup chopped walnuts
½ cup nondairy milk (such as coconut milk)
Freshly grated nutmeg, for garnish

Directions:
Place a metal trivet or steam rack in the instant pot and pour in the water. Set the sweet potatoes on the trivet. Lock the lid.
Select pressure cook and cook at high pressure for almost 25 minutes. To ensure the sweet potatoes cook evenly, make sure they are all the same size.
While the sweet potatoes cook, in a suitable bowl, stir together the ghee, salt, nutmeg, walnuts, and milk. Set aside.
When cooking is complete, use a natural release for almost 10 minutes, then quick release any remaining pressure.
Remove the lid. Using potholders, remove the trivet and place it in a clean sink or on a cutting board to cool.
Gently pull off the skins from the cooked sweet potatoes and discard them.
Add the sweet potato flesh to the prepared mixture in the bowl. Using a large spoon or potato masher, mash the ingredients until combined. Garnish with sea salt or nutmeg.

NUTRITION: Calories 299; Fat 11.2g; Sodium 264mg; Carbs 44.9g; Fiber 7.2g; Sugars 2.3g; Protein 7.1g

Chai Pudding

Prep time: 5 minutes **Cook time:** 0 minutes **Servings:** 2

Ingredients:
½ cup 2 tablespoons canned coconut milk
½ teaspoon sweet spice blend
1 teaspoon pure maple syrup
2 tablespoons chia seeds

Directions:
In a small pot, over low heat, warm milk just until it achieves a liquid and uniform consistency.
In a suitable bowl or mason jar, combine milk, sweet spice blend, maple syrup, and chia seeds. Stir well to combine. Place in refrigerator with a tightfitting lid for at least 2 hours.
Remove from refrigerator and eat as is.

NUTRITION: Calories 284; Fat 23g; Sodium 14mg; Carbs 17.5g; Fiber 11.1g; Sugars 4g; Protein 6.1g

Chocolate Bark

Prep time: 10 minutes **Cook time:** 5 minutes **Servings:** 8

Ingredients:
2 cups dark chocolate chips (cacao or higher) ½ cup chopped dried figs
½ cup chopped pecans
½ teaspoon orange zest
½ teaspoon fennel seeds, crushed or chopped

Directions:
Layer a cookie sheet with parchment paper.
Fill a medium saucepan ⅓ of the way with water. Place a suitable bowl on top. It should fit securely, but bottom of bowl should not touch bottom of pot.
Place chocolate chips in bowl and melt, while stirring occasionally. (you can melt chocolate in the microwave.)
Once chocolate is smooth and melted, pour it onto cookie sheet. Spread with a spatula into a thin, even layer.
Sprinkle evenly with figs, pecans, orange zest, and fennel seeds, and place in refrigerator to set at least 2 hours or overnight.
Once set, break into pieces and serve.

NUTRITION: Calories 220; Fat 13.1g; Sodium 1mg; Carbs 29.1g; Fiber 2g; Sugars 22.2g; Protein 3.2g

Spicy Ramen Soup

Prep Time: 10 Minutes **Cooking Time:** 15 Minutes **Servings:** 4

Ingredients:
2 Tablespoons Sesame Seeds
8 Ounces Rice Noodles, Cooked
¼ Cup Cucumber, Sliced Thin
¼ Cup Scallion, Sliced
¼ Cup Cilantro, Fresh & chopped

2 Tablespoons Sesame Oil
1 Tablespoon Coconut Aminos
1 Tablespoon Ginger, Fresh, Grated & Peeled 2 Tablespoons Rice vinegar
1 Tablespoons Honey, Raw
1 Tablespoon Lime Juice, Fresh
1 Teaspoon Chili Powder

Directions:
Mix your sesame seeds, cucumber, scallion, noodles, cilantro, sesame oil, ginger, coconut aminos, vinegar, honey, chili powder and lime juice together.
Dive amount four soup bowls, and serve at room temperature.

NUTRITION: Calories: 663Kcal Proteins: 21g Carbohydrates: 115g Fat:28 g

Balsamic Chicken

Prep Time: 10 Minutes **Cooking Time**: 30 Minutes **Servings**: 4

Ingredients:
¼ Cup Balsamic Vinegar
2 Tablespoons Honey, Raw
1 Teaspoon Sea Salt
1 Shallot, Minced
4 Chicken Breasts, Boneless & Skinless

Directions:
Start by heating your oven to 350.
Combine your shallot, salt, honey and vinegar together in a nine by thirteeninch baking dish. Stir until the honey has dissolved. Add your chicken in, turning to coat.
Bake for twenty minutes, and allow it to rest for five minutes before serving.

NUTRITION: Calories: 230Kcal Proteins: 35g Carbohydrates: 12g Fat: 4g

Chickpea Curry

Prep Time: 10 Minutes **Cooking Time**: 30 Minutes **Servings**: 4

Ingredients:
2 White Onions, Small & Diced
2 Cloves Garlic, Minced
2 Tablespoons Avocado Oil
½ Cup Vegetable Broth
1 Red Bell Pepper, Chopped
½ Cup Cashews, Chopped Rough
½ Cup Golden Raisins
1 Apple, Diced
½ Teaspoon Sea Salt, Fine
1 Tablespoon Curry Powder
2 Cups Chickpeas, Cooked, Rinsed & Drained
½ Cup Whole Milk Yogurt, Plain

Directions:

Get out a large skillet, placing it over medium heat. Sauté your garlic and onion in avocado oil, cooking for two to three minutes.

Add in your bell pepper, and sauté for five minutes.

Stir in your salt, curry powder and broth. Bring it to a simmer.

Add your raisins, apple, and chickpeas. Cook for five minutes.

Stir in your cashews right before you turn off the heat, and then serve warm topped with yogurt.

NUTRITION: Calories: 30Kcal Proteins: 11g Carbohydrates: 55g Fat: 18g

Honey-Lime Chicken Drumsticks

Prep Time: 10 minutes   **Cook time**: 35 to 45 minutes   **Serves** 4 to 6

Ingredients:

6 chicken drumsticks
1 cup unsweetened coconut yogurt
½ cup extravirgin olive oil
Juice of 2 limes
2 garlic cloves, smashed
1 tablespoon raw honey
1 teaspoon salt
1 teaspoon ground cumin
½ teaspoon paprika
½ teaspoon ground turmeric
¼ teaspoon freshly ground black pepper
Olive oil cooking spray

Directions:

Place the chicken in a shallow baking dish.

In a small bowl, whisk together the yogurt, olive oil, lime juice, garlic, honey, salt, cumin, paprika, turmeric, and pepper until smooth.

Pour yogurt mixture over the chicken. Cover with plastic wrap and chill for 30 minutes or overnight. Preheat the oven to 375ºF (190ºC).

Line a rimmed baking sheet with aluminum foil and lightly grease it with cooking spray.

Remove the drumsticks from the marinade and place them on the prepared sheet. Discard the marinade.

Place the sheet in the preheated oven and bake the drumsticks for 25 to 35 minutes, or until they start to brown and are cooked through.

NUTRITION: Calories: 380   fat: 31g   protein: 19g   carbs: 9g   fiber: 2g   sugar: 5g   sodium: 686mg

Lemon and Mint Breezy Blueberry

Prep Time: 10 minutes   **Cook time**: 0 minutes   **Serves** 1

Ingredients:

Handful of mint
1 teaspoon chia seeds
1 tablespoon lemon juice

1 cup of coconut water
1 cup strawberries
1 cup blueberries

Directions:
Add in the listed ingredients to a blender
Blend until you have a smooth and creamy texture Serve chilled and enjoy!

NUTRITION: Calories: 169 Fat: 13g Protein: 6g Total Carbs: 11g Fiber: 10g Net Carbs: 1g

Spinach Soup with Gnocchi

Servings: 4 **Cooking Time**: 25 Minutes

Ingredients:
1 tsp olive oil
1 cup red bell peppers
Sea salt and pepper to taste
2 garlic cloves, minced
2 carrots, chopped
3 cups vegetable broth
1 cup gnocchi
¾ cup nondairy milk
¼ cup nutritional yeast
2 cups chopped spinach
¼ cup black olives, chopped
Croutons, for topping

Directions:
Heat the oil in a pot over medium heat. Place in bell peppers, garlic, carrots, and salt and cook for 5 minutes. Stir in broth. Bring to a boil.
Put in gnocchi, cook for 10 minutes. Add in spinach and cook for 5 minutes. Stir in milk, nutritional yeast, and olives. Top with croutons.

NUTRITION: Calories: 205;Fat: 7g;Protein: 7g;Carbs: 28g**.**

Meatballs

Prep Time: 10 minutes **Cooking Time**: 25 minutes **Serve**: 4

Ingredients:
2 lbs ground beef
½ tsp ground ginger
1 tbsp garlic, minced
¼ cup fresh cilantro, chopped
1 lime zest
Pepper
Salt

Directions:

Preheat the oven to 350 F.

Line baking sheet with parchment paper and set aside.

In a mixing bowl, mix meat, ginger, garlic, cilantro, lime zest, pepper, and salt until well combined.

Make small balls from the meat mixture, place them onto the prepared baking sheet, and bake for 2325 minutes.

Serve and enjoy.

NUTRITION: Calories 426 Fat 12 g Carbohydrates 2 g Sugar 0.1 g Protein 69 g Cholesterol 203 mg

Ginger Honey Pork Chops

Prep Time: 10 minutes **Cooking Time**: 15 minutes Serve: 6

Ingredients:

6 pork chops

2 tbsp Dijon mustard

½ cup honey

2 tbsp ginger, grated

Pepper

Salt

Directions:

Preheat the grill.

Mix honey, Dijon mustard, ginger, pepper, and salt in a small bowl.

Brush pork chops with honey mixture and place onto the hot grill, and cook for 56 minutes on each side.

Serve and enjoy.

NUTRITION: Calories 352 Fat 20.2 g Carbohydrates 28 g Sugar 23 g Protein 15 g Cholesterol 69 m

Quick & Juicy Lamb Chops

Prep Time: 10 minutes **Cooking Time**: 8 minutes **Serve**: 4

Ingredients:

1 ½ lbs lamb chops

1 tbsp coconut oil

½ tsp turmeric

3 garlic cloves, minced

1 tbsp Canola oil

¼ tsp paprika

1 tbsp fresh lime juice

1 ½ tsp sea salt

Directions:

Mixing lamb chops, oregano, paprika, turmeric, garlic, olive oil, lemon zest, lemon juice, and salt in a mixing bowl. Cover and place in refrigerator for 1 hour.

Melt coconut oil in a pan over medium heat.

Place marinated lamb chops in a pan and cook for 34 minutes on each side.

Serve and enjoy.

NUTRITION: Calories 386Fat 15 gCarbohydrates 4 g Sugar 0.5 g Protein 41 g Cholesterol 153 mg

Salmon and Feta Cheese en Papillote

Ingredients:
1 tablespoon English mustard
2 tablespoons white vinegar
½ tsp. honey
Coarse salt and freshly ground pepper
5 tablespoons extravirgin olive oil
4 pcs. of 4 oz. salmon fillets
20 to 24 thin asparagus spears, trimmed 12 cherry tomatoes, halved
20 green olives, pitted
4 artichoke hearts, steamed and quartered 8 basil leaves, torn
¾ cup feta cheese

Directions:
Preheat your oven to 350 degrees Fahrenheit Combine the mustard, vinegar, honey, pepper and salt
Slowly add in the olive oil to this mixture by whisking it.
Season the salmon with salt and pepper
Cut for pieces of parchment paper 16 by 18 inches.
Fold each sheet in half lengthwise.
Evenly divide the asparagus among the four pieces of parchment paper.
Place a salmon on top of each of them.
Drizzle 1 tablespoon of vinaigrette.
Cook the salmon with tomatoes, olives, artichokes, basil and feta cheese.
Add another tablespoon of vinaigrette
Fold the parchment paper in half and seal the edges off by crimping them.
Transfer to a baking sheet and roast for 27 minutes.
Pace the packets on a plate and cut an x mark on top to release the steam.

Salad

Chopped Thai Salad

Prep Time: 25 minutes   **Cook time**: 0 minutes   **Serves** 6

Dressing:
½ cup extravirgin olive oil
3 tablespoons filtered water
2 tablespoons coconut aminos
1 tablespoon apple cider vinegar
1 tablespoon freshly squeezed lime juice
1 tablespoon raw honey
1 teaspoon sesame oil
1 teaspoon garlic powder
Dash ground ginger

Salad:

2 cups shredded kale, stemmed and thoroughly washed 2 cups shredded napa cabbage
2 cups shredded red cabbage
4 scallions, sliced
1 cup shredded carrots
1 red bell pepper, julienned
1 yellow bell pepper, julienned
1 cucumber, julienned
½ cup fresh cilantro leaves, roughly chopped
½ cup cashews, roughly chopped

Make the Dressing: In a medium bowl, whisk the olive oil, water, coconut aminos, vinegar, lime juice, honey, sesame oil, garlic powder, and ginger
until combined. Set aside.

Make the Salad:
1. In a large bowl, mix the kale, napa cabbage, red cabbage, scallions, carrots, red bell pepper, yellow bell pepper, and cucumber. Top with the cilantro and cashews. Pour the dressing over the salad, toss well, and serve immediately.

NUTRITION:
Calories: 272 fat: 22g protein: 3g carbs: 16g fiber: 4g sugar: 7g sodium: 40mg

Healthy Tuna Salad

Prep Time: 10 minutes **Cooking Time**: 5 minutes **Serve**: 2

Ingredients:
6 oz can tuna, drained & flaked
1 fresh lime juice
2 tbsp unsweetened dried cranberries
1 tbsp Dijon mustard
2 tbsp onion, minced
3 tbsp mayonnaise
Pepper
Salt

Directions:
Add tuna and remaining ingredients into the bowl and mix until well combined.
Cover and place in the fridge for 1 hour.
Serve and enjoy.

NUTRITION: Calories 117 Fat 5 g Carbohydrates 2 g Sugar 8 g
Protein 13 g Cholesterol 17 mg

Massaged Swiss Chard Salad with Chopped Egg

Prep Time: 25 minutes **Cook time**: 0 minutes Serves 4

Dressing:
¼ cup olive oil

3 tablespoons freshly squeezed lemon juice
2 teaspoons raw honey
1 teaspoon Dijon mustard
Sea salt, to taste

Salad:
5 cups chopped Swiss chard
3 large hardboiled eggs, peeled and chopped
1 English cucumber, diced
½ cup sliced radishes
½ cup chopped pecans
For the Dressing:

In a bowl, whisk the olive oil, lemon juice, honey, and mustard. Season with salt and set it aside.
For the Salad:
In a bowl, toss the Swiss chard and dressing together for about 4 minutes, or until the greens start to soften. Divide the greens evenly among four plates. Top each salad with egg, cucumber, radishes, and pecans.

NUTRITION: Calories: 241   fat: 21g   protein: 7g   carbs: 9g   fiber: 2g   sugar: 5g   sodium: 163mg

Veggie Salad

Prep time: 10 minutes. **Cooking time:** 0 minutes. **Servings:** 4
Ingredients:
2 Carrots, peeled and grated
1 avocado, pitted, peeled, and chopped
½ green cabbage head, shredded
2 Strawberries, halved
Salt and black pepper to taste
¼ teaspoon matcha powder
1 teaspoon maple syrup
¼ Tablespoon white wine vinegar
1 tablespoon Dijon mustard
¼ cup lemon juice
¾ cup olive oil

Directions:
1. In a bowl, whisk together the lemon juice with oil, vinegar, matcha tea powder, maple syrup, mustard, salt, and pepper. In a salad bowl, mix avocado with cabbage, strawberries, and carrots.
2. Add lemon juice, oil, vinegar, matcha powder, maple syrup, mustard, salt, and pepper. Toss well and serve for lunch.
3. Enjoy!

NUTRITION: Calories: 211 Fat: 4 g Fiber: 2 g Carbs: 8 g Protein: 7g

Grilled Eggplant Salad

Prep time: 10 minutes. **Cooking time:** 20 minutes. **Servings:** 4

Ingredients:
1 tomato, diced
1 eggplant, pricked
A pinch of salt and black pepper
¼ teaspoon ground turmeric
1(½) teaspoon red wine vinegar
½ teaspoon chopped oregano
½ tablespoon olive oil
2 garlic cloves, minced
½ tablespoon chopped parsley
½ Tablespoon chopped capers

Directions:
1. Preheat your grill over medium-high heat, then add the eggplant and cook for 15 minutes, flipping occasionally. Scoop the flesh, roughly slice it, and place it in a bowl. Toss tomatoes, turmeric, garlic, vinegar, oregano, parsley, oil, capers with salt, and pepper to taste. Enjoy!

NUTRITION: Calories: 192 Fat: 7 g Fiber: 6 g Carbs: 12 g Protein: 7 g

Blackberry Salad

Prep time: 5 minutes. **Cooking time:** 0 minutes. **Servings:** 1

Ingredients:
¼ cup sliced almonds
¼ cup blackberries
¼ cup strawberries, halved
1 banana, peeled and sliced
Ground cinnamon, a pinch

Directions:
1. In a bowl, mix the blackberries with strawberries, cinnamon, banana, and almonds. Serve for breakfast.
2. Enjoy!

NUTRITION: Calories: 90 Fat: 0.3 g Fiber: 1 g Carbs: 0 g Protein: 5 g

Zucchini Salad

Prep time: 10 minutes. **Cooking time:** 0 minutes. **Servings:** 4

Ingredients:
2 Zucchinis, spiralized
1 cup beets, baked, peeled, and grated
½ bunch kale, chopped
½ tablespoon olive oil
For the tahini sauce:
1 tablespoon maple syrup
Juice of 1 lime

¼ inch fresh ginger, grated
$^1/_3$ cup sesame seed paste

Directions:
 Combine the zucchinis, beets, kale, and oil in a salad dish. Whisk together the maple syrup, lime juice, ginger, and sesame paste in a separate small bowl. Toss the salad with the dressing and serve for breakfast.

NUTRITION: Calories: 183 Fat: 3 g Fiber: 2 g Carbs: 7 g Protein: 9 g

Nutritious Salad With Lentil And Beets

Servings: 4 **Cooking Time:** 0 Minute

Ingredients:
4 cups baby spinach
15 ounces can lentils, drained and rinsed 4 cooked peeled beets, 1 cut into 8 pieces 1 small red onion, sliced
cup extra-virgin olive oil
1 tablespoon apple cider vinegar
1 teaspoon salt
¼ teaspoon black pepper, freshly ground

Directions:
1. Arrange the spinach leaves on a serving platter or in a bowl.
2. Top with the lentils, beets, and red onion.
3. Whisk together the olive oil, cider vinegar, salt, and pepper in a small bowl.
4. Drizzle the salad with the dressing and serve.

NUTRITION:
Per Serving: Calories: 320 ;Fat: 18g ;Protein: 11g ;Carbs: 29g .

Carrot and Raisin Salad

Prep Time: 12 minutes   **Cook time**: 0 minutes   **Serves** 6

4 cups shredded carrots
1 cup raisins, chopped
¾ cup sunflower seeds
¼ cup maple syrup, plus additional as needed
¼ cup freshly squeezed lemon juice, plus additional as needed In a large bowl, mix together the carrots, raisins, and sunflower seeds.
Stir in the maple syrup and lemon juice. Taste, and add more lemon juice or maple syrup if necessary.

NUTRITION: Calories: 173   fat: 3g   protein: 3g   carbs: 37g   fiber: 3g   sugar: 26g   sodium: 57mg

Pineapple Apple Salad

Prep Time: 10 minutes **Cooking Time**: 5 minutes **Serve**: 4

Ingredients:

1 cup crushed pineapple, drained
2 cups coconut yogurt
¾ cup walnuts, chopped
½ cup raisins
¼ cup celery, diced
4 medium apples, chopped

Directions:
Add crushed pineapple and remaining ingredients into the mixing bowl and mix well.
Serve and enjoy.

NUTRITION: Calories 343 Fat 14 g Carbohydrates 53 g Sugar 39 g Protein 6 g Cholesterol 0 mg

Perfect Chicken Salad

Prep Time: 10 minutes **Cooking Time**: 5 minutes **Serve**: 4

Ingredients:
For salad:
2 cups cooked chicken, shredded
¼ cup raisins
1 green onion, chopped
1 cup shredded cabbage
1 cup shredded carrots
For dressing:
1/3 cup olive oil
2 tbsp apple cider vinegar
1 tsp honey
1 garlic clove, minced
1 tbsp tahini
1 tsp turmeric
¼ tsp kosher salt

Directions:
Add all salad ingredients into the large bowl and mix well.
In a small bowl, whisk together dressing ingredients, pour over salad, and toss well.
Serve and enjoy.

NUTRITION: Calories 326 Fat 21 g Carbohydrates 11 g Sugar 9 g Protein 28 g Cholesterol 54 mg

Stone Fruit Salad

Prep Time: 15 minutes. **Cooking time**: 0 minutes. **Servings:** 6

Ingredients:
2 Cup mixed chopped greens
1 cup sliced fresh peaches
1 cup fresh cherries, pitted and halved
1 cup sliced fresh nectarines
½ cup pecans, chopped
¼ cup thinly sliced red onion

¼ cup fresh basil leaves
$^1/_3$ cup extravirgin olive oil
¼ cup balsamic vinegar
1 tablespoon freshly squeezed lemon juice
½ tablespoon raw honey
Dash salt
Freshly ground black pepper to taste

Directions:
In a large bowl, gently combine the greens, peaches, cherries, nectarines, pecans, red onion, and basil.
In a small bowl, add olive oil, vinegar, lemon juice, honey, and salt, season with pepper, and whisk to combine.
Pour the dressing over the salad and gently toss to combine. Serve immediately.

NUTRITION: Calories: 235 Fat: 19 g Protein: 2 g Carbs: 16 g Fiber: 3 g Sugar: 9 g Sodium: 87 mg

WatermelonCucumber Salad

Prep Time: 25 minutes. **Cooking time:** 0 minutes. **Servings**: 4

Ingredients:

Dressing:
½ cup olive oil
¼ cup apple cider vinegar
¼ Tablespoon raw honey
1 teaspoon freshly grated lemon zest (optional) Pinch sea salt

Salad:
Cup (½inch) watermelon cubes
1 English cucumber, cut into ½inch cubes
1 cup halved snow peas
1 scallion, white and green parts, chopped
Cup shredded kale
1 tablespoon chopped fresh cilantro

Directions:

Make the dressing: In a small bowl, whisk the olive oil, cider vinegar, honey, and lemon zest (if using). Season with sea salt and set it aside.

Make the salad: In a large bowl, toss together the watermelon, cucumber, snow peas, scallion, and dressing.
Divide the kale among 4 plates and top with the watermelon mixture.
Serve garnished with cilantro.

NUTRITION: Calories: 353 Fat: 26 g Protein: 4 g Carbs: 30 g Fiber: 3 g Sugar: 19 g Sodium: 7 mg

Tarragon Scallops

Servings: 1 **Cooking Time**: 10 Minutes

Ingredients:
2 garlic cloves, minced
1 red chili, minced
8 king scallops
1 tbsp olive oil
Juice of ½ lime
2 tbsp chopped tarragon

Directions:
Warm the olive oil in a skillet over medium heat and fry scallops for about 1 minute per side until lightly golden. Add the chopped chili and garlic cloves to the pan and squeeze the lime juice over the scallops.
Saute for 23 minutes. Sprinkle the tarragon over the top and serve.

NUTRITION:
Calories: 235;Fat: 15g;Protein: 15g;Carbs: 13g.

Especial Glazed Salmon

Prep Time: 45minutes **Total time**: 55minutes **Yield**: 4servings

Ingredients:
4 pieces salmon fillets, 5 oz.
4 tbsps. coconut aminos
each
4 tsp. olive oil
2 tsp. ginger, minced
4 tsp. garlic, minced
2 tbsp. sugarfree ketchup
4 tbsps. dry white wine
2 tbsps. red boat fish sauce, low sodium

Directions:
Take a bowl and mix in coconut aminos, garlic, ginger, fish sauce, and mix.
Add salmon and let it marinate for 1520minutes. Take a skillet/pan and place it over medium heat. Add oil and let it heat up. Add salmon fillets and cook on HIGH for 34minutes per side. Remove dish once crispy. Add sauce and wine. Simmer for 5minutes on low heat. Return salmon to the glaze and flip until both sides are glazed. Serve and enjoy!

NUTRITION: Calories: 372 Fat: 24g Carbohydrates: 3g Protein: 35g

Tuna and Kale

Prep Time: 5 minutes **Cooking Time**: 20 minutes **Servings**: 4

Ingredients

1 pound tuna fillets, boneless, skinless and cubed A pinch of salt and black pepper
2 tablespoons olive oil
1 cup kale, torn
½ cup cherry tomatoes, cubed
1 yellow onion, chopped

Directions

Heat up a pan with the oil over medium heat, add the onion and sauté for 5 minutes.
Add the tuna and the other ingredients, toss, cook everything for 15
minutes more, divide between plates and serve.

NUTRITION: Calories: 251Fat: 4Fiber: 7Carbs: 14Protein: 7

Veggie, Salmon & Quinoa Bowl

Servings: 4 **Cooking Time**: 15 Minutes

Ingredients:

½ cup toasted slivered almonds
1 lb cooked salmon, flaked
4 cups cooked quinoa
6 radishes, thinly sliced
1 zucchini, cut into halfmoons
3 cups arugula
1 red onion, sliced thin
½ cup almond oil
1 tsp sugarfree hot sauce
1 tbsp apple cider vinegar
1 tsp sea salt

Directions:

Stir the flaked salmon, cooked quinoa, radishes, zucchini, arugula, and red onion in a large bowl. Pour
in the almond oil, hot sauce, apple cider vinegar, and sea salt and toss to combine. Divide the mixture
between four bowls. Top with slivered almonds and serve immediately.

NUTRITION: Per Serving: Calories: 770;Fat: 50g;Protein: 38g;Carbs: 45g.

Baked Cod Fillets With Mushroom

Servings: 4 **Cooking Time**: 30 Minutes

Ingredients:

8 oz shiitake mushrooms, sliced
1 ½ lb cod fillets
1 leek, sliced thin

Sea salt and pepper to taste
1 lemon, zested
2 tbsp extravirgin olive oil
1 tbsp coconut aminos
1 tsp sweet paprika
½ cup vegetable broth

Directions:
Preheat your oven to 375ºF. In a baking dish, combine the olive oil, leek, mushrooms, coconut aminos, lemon zest, paprika, and salt. Place the cod fillets over and sprinkle it with salt and pepper. Pour in the vegetable broth. Bake for 1520 minutes, or until the cod is firm but cooked through. Serve and enjoy!

NUTRITION: Calories: 220;Fat: 5g;Protein: 32g;Carbs: 12g.

Broiled Sea Bass
Servings: 2

Ingredients:
2 minced garlic cloves
Pepper
1 tablespoon lemon juice
2 white sea bass fillets
¼ teaspoon herb seasoning blend

Directions:
Spray a broiler pan with some olive oil and place the fillets on it.
Sprinkle the lemon juice, garlic and the spices over the fillets.
Broil for about 10 min or until the fish is golden.
Serve over a bed of sautéed spinach if desired.

NUTRITION: Calories: 169, Fat:3 g, Carbs:0.34 g, Protein:13 g, Sugars:0.2 g, Sodium:323 mg

Greek Baked Cod
Prep Time: 10 minutes **Cooking time**: 15 minutes **Servings**: 4
Add a little of the Mediterranean touch to your meal.

Ingredients:
1 ½ lb. cod fillet pieces (4–6 pieces)
5 garlic cloves, peeled and minced
¼ C. fresh parsley leaves, chopped
Lemon Juice Mixture:
5 tbsp. fresh lemon juice
5 tbsp. extra virgin olive oil
2 tbsp. vegan butter, melted
For coating:

⅓ C. allpurpose flour
1 tsp. coriander, ground
¾ tsp. sweet Spanish paprika
¾ tsp. cumin, ground
¾ tsp. salt
½ tsp. black pepper

Directions:
Preheat oven to 400°F.
Mix lemon juice, olive oil, and melted butter, set aside.
In another shallow bowl, mix allpurpose flour, spices, salt, and pepper, set next to the lemon bowl to create a station.
Pat the fish fillet dry, then dip the fish in the lemon juice mixture then dip it in the flour mixture, and brush off extra flour.
In a castiron skillet over mediumhigh heat, add 2 tbsp. olive oil.
Once heated, add in the fish and sear on each side for color but do not thoroughly cook, then remove from heat.
With the remaining lemon juice mixture, add the minced garlic and mix.
Drizzle all over the fish fillets.
Bake for 10 minutes, until it begins to flake easily with a fork.
Allow the dish to cool completely.
Distribute among the containers, store for 2–3 days.
To serve: reheat in the microwave for 1–2 minutes or until heated through. Sprinkle chopped parsley over. Enjoy!

NUTRITION: Calories: 3804 kcal Fat: 26 g Protein: 323 g Carbs: 16 g Sodium: 629 mg

Mussels and Clams in White Wine

Prep Time: 10 minutes **Cooking time**: 10 minutes **Servings**: 4

Shellfish are loaded with healthy proteins that help you manage excess weight and improve your immune function.

Ingredients:
2 tbsp. extravirgin olive oil
1 shallot, minced
2 garlic cloves, minced
1 C. dry white wine
½ tsp. red pepper flakes
1lb. clams, scrubbed
1lb. mussels, scrubbed and debearded
¼ C. arugula, chopped

Directions:

In a large, deep skillet, heat the olive oil over low heat. Cook the shallot for about 5 minutes, until it starts to soften. Add the garlic and cook for 1 minute.

Stir in the white wine and red pepper flakes and cook for 1 minute to allow the alcohol to evaporate. Increase the heat to medium and add the clams and mussels.

Cover and steam for 3–5 minutes until the shellfish have opened.

Discard any that do not open. If you need more liquid to steam them, add some water.

Remove the shellfish from the pan and top with the sauce from the pan and chopped arugula.

Variation tip: You can enjoy this dish as is, or serve it over linguine if you like.

NUTRITION: Calories: 1897 kcal Total Fat: 79 g Saturated Fat: 28 g Protein: 39 g Total Carbohydrates: 77 g Fiber: 0.32 g Sugar: 0.56 g Cholesterol: 24 mg

Spicy Cod
Servings: 4

Ingredients:
 2 tablespoons Fresh chopped parsley
 2 lbs. cod fillets
 2 c. low sodium salsa
 1 tablespoon flavorless oil

Directions:
 Preheat the oven to 350◦F.
 In a large, deep baking dish drizzle the oil along the bottom. Place the cod fillets in the dish. Pour the salsa over the fish. Cover with foil for 20 minutes. Remove the foil last 10 minutes of cooking.
 Bake in the oven for 20 – 30 minutes, until the fish is flaky.
 Serve with white or brown rice. Garnish with parsley.

NUTRITION: Calories: 110, Fat:11 g, Carbs:83 g, Protein:15 g, Sugars:0 g, Sodium:122 mg

Creamy Turmeric Shrimp
Prep Time: 10 minutes Cooking Time: 8 minutes Serve: 4

Ingredients:
1 lb shrimp
1 tbsp cornstarch
1/8 tsp cayenne
1 tsp olive oil
2 tsp turmeric
14 oz can coconut milk
Salt

Directions:
Heat oil in a pan over medium heat.
Add shrimp to the pan and cook until shrimp turns pink in color.

Remove from pan and set aside.

Add milk, cayenne, turmeric, and salt to the same pan and stir well.

Stir cornstarch with ¼ cup water, add it to the pan and continue until sauce thickens.

Add shrimp and stir well.

Serve and enjoy.

NUTRITION: Calories 352 Fat 24 g Carbohydrates 1 g Sugar 0.1 g Protein 29 g Cholesterol 239 mg

Salmon Balls

Prep Time: 6minutes   **Total time:** 19minutes   **Yield:** 2servings

Ingredients:

Salt and ground black pepper to

2 tbsp. water

taste

2 tbsp. lemon juice

½ tsp dried cilantro

½ tsp paprika

½ tsp ginger powder

3 tbsp. coconut oil

½ c. heavy cream

1 garlic clove

1 egg

1 avocado

2 tbsp. keto mayo

1 can of tuna

Directions:

Drain the salmon, chop it. Mince the garlic clove, peel the avocado. In a bowl, Mix the garlic, egg, mayo, and fish, season with salt, paprika, and ginger, mix well. Make 4 balls of it. Using a skillet, preheat the oil at medium heat. Fry the balls for 46minutes on each side.

Meanwhile, put the lemon juice, cilantro, avocado, heavy cream, and 1 tbsp.

Of oil in a blender. Pulse well.

Serve the balls with the sauce.

NUTRITION: Carbs: 3,9 g Fats: 50 g Protein: 20,1 g Calories: 555

Cod and Mushrooms Mix

Prep Time: 10 minutes **Cooking time**: 25 minutes **Servings**: 4

This delectable recipe adds some earthiness to your meal and nutrients to your body.

Ingredients:

2 cod fillets, boneless

4 tbsp. olive oil

4 oz. mushrooms, sliced

Sea salt and black pepper to taste

12 cherry tomatoes, halved

8 oz. lettuce leaves, torn

1 avocado, pitted, peeled, and cubed
1 red chili pepper, chopped
1 tbsp. cilantro, chopped
2 tbsp. balsamic vinegar
1oz. feta cheese, crumbled

Directions:
Put the fish in a roasting pan, brush it with 2 tbsp. oil, sprinkle salt and pepper all over and broil under mediumhigh heat for 15
minutes.
Meantime, heat up a pan with the rest of the oil over medium heat; add the mushrooms, stir, and sauté for 5 minutes.
Now add the rest of the ingredients, toss, cook for 5 minutes more, and divide between plates.
Top with the fish and serve right away.

NUTRITION: Calories: 2869 kcal Fat: 20.7 g Fiber: 67 g carbs: 45 g Protein: 137 g

Creamy Sea Bass Mix

Servings: 4

Ingredients:
1 tablespoon chopped parsley
2 tablespoons avocado oil
1 c. coconut cream
1 tablespoon lime juice
1 chopped yellow onion
¼ teaspoon black pepper
4 boneless sea bass fillets

Directions:
Heat up a pan with the oil over medium heat, add the onion, toss and sauté for 2
minutes.
Add the fish and cook it for 4 minutes on each side.
Add the rest of the ingredients, cook everything for 4 minutes more, divide between plates and serve.

NUTRITION: Calories: 283, Fat:13 g, Carbs:15 g, Protein:8 g, Sugars:6 g, Sodium:508 mg

Dessert and Smothie

Tropical Popsicles

Prep Time: 10 Minutes **Cooking Time**: 10Minutes Servings: 6

Ingredients:
2 Kiwi, sliced
3 cups Pineapple, chopped

2 tbsp. Coconut Oil

2 tsp. Turmeric

½ tsp. Black Pepper

Directions:

First, place all the ingredients to make the popsicles excluding the kiwi in a highspeed blender for 2 minutes or until you get a smooth mixture.

Next, pour the smoothie into the popsicle molds.

After that, insert the kiwi slices into the molds and then place the frames in the freezer until set.

NUTRITION: Calories: 101 Kcal Protein: 0.5g Carbohydrates: 15g Fat:4g

Mango & Kale Smoothie

Prep time: 15 minutes **Cooking Time:** 20 minutes **Servings:** 1

Ingredients:

1 cup baby kale

1 cup frozen mango chunks

1 small banana, sliced

1 cup fresh orange juice

Directions:

Combine the kale, mango, banana, and orange juice in a blender. Blend on medium-low speed, scraping down the sides as needed until well blended.

Increase the speed to medium-high and blend until the mixture is extremely smooth.

Fancy Cold Soup Smoothie

Servings: 1 **Cooking Time**: 15 Minutes

Ingredients:

Frozen Veggie Mix:

2 cups butternut squash, diced

1 cup broccoli florets

1 cup onions, diced

4 cloves garlic, peeled

3 cups water

Smoothie:

1 bag steamed and then frozen mixed veggies 1½ cups bone broth or water

2 tablespoons collagen peptides

1 tablespoon MCT oil or MCT oil powder

2 teaspoons apple cider vinegar

½ teaspoon thyme or oregano, dried

½ teaspoon Himalayan salt, fine

½ teaspoon turmeric powder

Directions:

1. Make the frozen veggie mix. Place all of the veggies in a large skillet with a tight-fitting lid. Add the water and bring to a boil. Cover and steam for 15 minutes or until the butternut squash is fork-tender. Remove from the heat, drain, and let cool.

2. Divide the cooled vegetables into five resealable plastic bags, about 1

cup per bag. Seal and pop in the freezer for 1 hour before making your smoothie.

3. Place 1 bag of frozen veggies in a blender when you're ready to make a smoothie and add the smoothie ingredients then blend until smooth.

Drink. Store any leftovers in the fridge in an airtight container for up to 4 days.

NUTRITION: Per Serving: Calories: 304 ;Fat: 18g ;Protein: 20g;Carbs: 9g.

Almond Butter Chocolate Cups

Prep Time: 10 minutes   **Cook time**: 5 minutes   **Makes** 9 cups 6 ounces (170 g) dark chocolate, chopped

Ingredients:
½ cup natural almond butter
2 tablespoons raw honey
½ teaspoon vanilla extract
Dash salt

Directions:
Line 9 cups of a mini muffin tin with mini paper liners.

In a small saucepan over low heat, slowly melt the chocolate. Use half of the chocolate among the mini muffin cups. Set the rest of the chocolate aside.

In a small bowl, stir together the almond butter, honey, and vanilla.

Divide the mixture into 9 portions and roll each into a small ball. Drop 1
ball into each muffin cup.

Drizzle the remaining chocolate into each cup, covering the almond butter balls.

Sprinkle each lightly with the salt.

Refrigerate until solid.

NUTRITION: calories: 193   fat: 16g   protein: 5g   carbs: 14g   fiber: 0g   sugar: 9g   sodium: 22mg

Vanilla Cookies with Chocolate Chips

Prep Time: 15 minutes   **Cook time:** 10 minutes   **Makes** 12 cookies ¾ cup creamy almond butter

Ingredients:
½ cup coconut sugar
¼ cup cocoa powder
2 teaspoons vanilla extract
1 egg
1 egg yolk
1 teaspoon baking soda
¼ teaspoon salt
½ cup semisweet chocolate chips
Dash sea salt (optional)

Directions:
Preheat the oven to 350ºF (180ºC).

Line 2 baking sheets with parchment paper.

In a medium bowl, cream together the almond butter, coconut sugar, cocoa powder, and vanilla.

In a small bowl, whisk the egg and egg yolk. Add the eggs to the almond butter mixture and stir to combine.

Stir in the baking soda, salt, and chocolate chips until well mixed. Divide the dough into 12 pieces. Roll the dough into balls and put 6 on each prepared pan.

Bake for 9 to 10 minutes. Let the cookies rest on the pans for 5 minutes, where they'll continue to cook. Sprinkle each with a dash of sea salt (if using). Remove to a cooling rack.

NUTRUTION: Calories: 307 fat: 20g protein: 9g carbs: 28g fiber: 4g sugar: 20g sodium: 364mg

Mango, Cucumber and Spinach Smoothie

Prep time: 10-minutes   **Total time:** 10-minutes   **Yield:** 1 serving

Ingredients:
1 c. water
1 c. orange juice, fresh
3 c. baby spinach
1 c. frozen mango, cubed and
deseeded
2 apples, cored and chopped
1 cucumber, ends removed and chopped
roughly roughly

Directions:
Add all ingredients to a blender. Blend until smooth and creamy. Serve and enjoy.
NUTRITION: Calories 455 Fat 2g Carbs 111g Protein 8g Sugar: 21g Fiber 15g Sodium 90mg

Apple Muesli

Servings: 4 To 6 **Cooking Time**: 0 Minutes

Ingredients:
- 2 cups gluten-free rolled oats
- ¼ cup no-added-sugar apple juice
- 1¾ cups coconut milk
- 1 tablespoon apple cider vinegar
- 1 apple, cored and chopped
- Dash ground cinnamon

Directions:
1. Combine the oats, apple juice, coconut milk, and apple cider vinegar in a bowl.
Stir to mix well. Wrap the bowl in plastic and refrigerate overnight.
2. Remove the bowl from the refrigerator. Top with apple and sprinkle with cinnamon, then serve.

NUTRITION: calories: 212 ; fat: 3.7g ; protein: 6.1g ; carbs: 38.9g ; fiber: 6.0g ; sugar: 10.0g ; sodium: 73mg

Carrot Cake

Servings: 6 Cooking Time: 0 Minutes

Ingredients:
- 1 cup pineapple, dried and chopped
- 2 carrots, chopped
- 1 ½ cups coconut flour

- 1 cup dates, pitted
- ½ cup shredded coconut, unsweetened
- ½ teaspoon ground cinnamon

Directions:
1. Put carrots in your food processor, pulse then add the flour, dates, pineapple, coconut and cinnamon. Pulse again and spoon this into a cake pan, spread evenly and keep in the freezer for 3 hours before serving.
2. Enjoy!

NUTRITION: calories 160, fat 7, fiber 4, carbs 11, protein 4.

Lemony Steamed Asparagus

Servings: 4 **Cooking Time:** 0 Minutes

Ingredients:
1pound asparagus, woody ends removed Juice from
½ large lemon
¼ teaspoon kosher salt

Directions:
Add ½ cup water to the inner pot and add the steam rack. Add the asparagus to the steamer basket and place the basket on top of the rack, then steam within 1 minute.
Transfer, and top with lemon juice and salt.

NUTRITION: Calories 13 Fat: 0g Protein: 1g Sodium: 146mg Fiber: 1g Carbohydrates: 3g Sugar: 1g

Spiced Tea Pudding

Prep Time: 10minutes   **Total time:** 20minutes   **Yield:** 3servings

Ingredients:
1 can coconut milk
½ c. coconut flakes
1 c. almond milk
1 tsp. nutmeg
1 tbsp. Ground cinnamon
½ tsp. cloves
1 tsp. allspice
1 tbsp. Raw honey
tsps. ground ginger
1 tsp. Cardamom
tbsps. pumpkin seeds
1 ½ c. berries
1 tbsp. chia seeds
1 tsp. green tea powder

Directions:
Puree tea powder with coconut milk, almond milk, cinnamon, coconut flakes, nutmeg, allspice, cloves, honey, cardamom, and ginger in your blender, then divide into bowls. Heat a pan over medium heat,

add berries until bubbling, then transfer to your blender and pulse well. Divide the berries into the bowls with the coconut milk mix, top with chia seeds and pumpkin seeds and serve.

NUTRITION: Calories 150, Fat 6, Fiber 5, Carbs 14, Protein 8

Fresh Peach Smoothie

Servings: 2 Cooking Time: 5 Minutes

Ingredients:
1 avocado
2 cups baby spinach
1 cup peach chunks
2 cups almond milk
Juice of 1 lime
2 tbsp maple syrup

Directions:
In a food processor, combine avocado, spinach, pear, milk, lime, and maple syrup. Purée until smooth to serve.

NUTRITION: Per Serving: Calories: 886;Fat: 77g;Protein: 9g;Carbs: 53.9g.

Delicious Cherry Smoothie

Prep time: 10 minutes **Cooking Time:** 5 minutes **Serve:** 2

Ingredients:
¾ cup cherries pitted
½ cup water
¼ cup cherry juice
1 cup unsweetened almond milk
½ cup strawberries
½ cup raspberries
1 cup pineapple chunks
Directions:
Add cherries and remaining ingredients into the blender and blend until smooth and creamy. Serve immediately and enjoy.

NUTRITION: Calories 225 Fat 8 g Carbohydrates 33 g Sugar 11.9 g Protein 5 g Cholesterol 0 mg

Avocado Sorbet

Prep time: 5 minutes **Cooking time:** 10 minutes **Servings:** 4

If you do not like the bland taste of avocados, this is a recipe you will fall in love with.
Ingredients:
4 tbsp maple syrup
1 C. water
1 tsp. lime zest, grated
1 tbsp. honey
2 ripe avocados, pitted and skin removed
2 tbsp. lime juice

Directions:

Combine together the syrup and water in a small pan over medium flame.

Stir until the syrup dissolves completely, and then remove from the flame.

Place the avocados in the food processor. Add the syrup with the honey, lime zest, and lime juice into the food processor.

Process it until it reaches a smooth consistency.

Place the mix into a baking pan and cover with foil. Place the mix into the freezer until completely frozen.

Serve in ice cream bowls and enjoy.

NUTRITION: Calories: 158.19 kcal Carbohydrates: 23 g Fats: 8.16 g Protein: 1.18 g

Other wonderful recipes

Parsley with Avocado Chicken Soup

Prep Time: 15 minutes   **Cook time:** 35 minutes   **Serves** 4

Ingredients:

4 tablespoons avocado oil

¼ cup carrots, chopped into ½inch pieces

½ cup celery, chopped into ½inch pieces

½ cup yellow onion, diced

2 cloves garlic, minced

6 cups Chicken Bone Broth (storebought or homemade) 1½ tablespoons chopped fresh parsley

1 bay leaf

1 teaspoon salt

8 skinless, boneless chicken thighs

1 (14 ounce) can fullfat coconut milk

1 tablespoon coconut flour

2 avocados, diced

Directions:

In a large pot, heat the oil over medium heat. Add the carrot, celery, and onion, and sauté for about 4 minutes until soft.

Add the garlic and sauté for another minute.

Add the bone broth, parsley, bay leaf, salt, and chicken thighs to the pot.

Bring to a boil, then cover with a lid and reduce the heat to low and let it simmer for 10 to 15 minutes or until the chicken is cooked through.

Remove the chicken and allow it to cool for 5 minutes before shredding it using two forks.

In a small saucepan, combine the coconut milk and coconut flour over medium heat and cook for 5 minutes.

Whisk the coconut milk mixture into the soup.

Return the shredded chicken to the soup and stir to combine. Let simmer for 5 more minutes.

Top with the diced avocado just before serving.

NUTRITION: Calories: 626   Fat: 50g   Protein: 28g   Total Carbs: 16g   Fiber: 8g   Net Carbs: 8g

Trout Fillets With Almond Crust

Servings: 4 **Cooking Time:** 20 Minutes

Ingredients:
½ cup wholewheat breadcrumbs
2 trout fillets
1 tbsp extravirgin olive oil
1 tsp Italian seasoning
1 lemon, juiced and zested
½ cup chopped almonds

Directions:
Preheat your oven to 375ºF. Mix breadcrumbs, Italian seasoning, lemon zest, lemon juice, and half of the almonds in a shallow dish.
Lay the fillets skin side down onto the oiled baking tray and then flip over so that both sides of your fish are coated in the oil. Roll the fillets into the nut mixture on both sides to coat. Return to the baking tray. Bake for 67 minutes on each side and serve.

NUTRITION: Per Serving: Calories: 870;Fat: 50g;Protein: 51g;Carbs: 56g.

Avocado Spinach Dip

Prep Time: 5s minutes **Cooking Time**: 5 minutes **Serve:** 6

Ingredients:
1 avocado, scoop out the flesh
4 1/2 cups baby spinach
3 garlic cloves
1 ½ tbsp fresh lime juice
1 small onion, chopped
Salt

Directions:
Add spinach and remaining ingredients into the blender and blend until smooth.
Serve and enjoy.

NUTRITION: Calories 79 Fat 7 g Carbohydrates 7 g Sugar 0.6 g Protein 5 g Cholesterol 0 mg

Poultry And Meats Lamb Shanks Braised Under Pressure

Servings: 4 **Cooking Time:** 50 Minutes

Ingredients:
46 lamb shanks
3 carrots, sliced
2 tomatoes, quartered

1 garlic clove, crushed
1 tbsp chopped oregano
¾ cup wholewheat flour
8 tsp olive oil
1 onion, chopped
¾ cup red wine
¼ cup beef broth

Directions:
Place ¼ cup of flour and lamb shanks in a plastic bag. Shake until you coat the shanks well. Discard the excess flour. Heat 4 tsp of the oil in your Instant Pot on "Sauté". Brown the shanks on both sides. Set aside.
Heat the remaining olive oil and sauté the onions, garlic, and carrots for a couple of minutes. Stir in tomatoes, wine, broth, and oregano.
Return the shanks to the cooker. Seal the lid and cook for 25 minutes on "Manual". Once ready, perform a quick pressure release. Whisk together the remaining flour and 8 tsp of cold water. Stir this mixture into the lamb sauce and cook with the lid off until it thickens. Serve and enjoy!

NUTRITION: Calories: 800;Fat: 43g;Protein: 73g;Carbs: 20g.

Baked Zucchini Fries

Prep Time: 10 Minutes **Cooking Time:** 20 Minutes **Servings:** 12

Ingredients:
½ cup almond flour
½ teaspoon salt
½ teaspoon garlic powder
½ teaspoon freshly ground black pepper
1 medium zucchini, trimmed and halved width wise 1 tablespoon avocado oil

Directions:
Preheat the oven to 425°F.
Line a baking sheet with aluminium foil.
In a small bowl, mix the almond flour, salt, garlic powder, and pepper.
Cut each zucchini half into about 6 strips that resemble fries. Brush the strips with the avocado oil, and roll in the almond flour mixture until well coated. Evenly space the fries on the prepared pan.
Bake for 20 minutes, or until crispy.
COOKING TIP: These zucchini fries do not save well and lose their crunch when refrigerated. You can cut the zucchini strips and prepare the almond flour mixture ahead of time, but coating the zucchini strips and baking them should be done just before serving.

NUTRITION: Calories: 230Kcal Proteins: 6g Carbohydrates: 7g Fat: 21g

Mushroom Squash with Vegetable Soup

Prep Time: 10 minutes **Cook time:** 45 minutes **Serves** 2

Ingredients:
15 dried shiitake mushrooms, soaked in water

6 cups low salt vegetable stock
½ butternut squash, peeled and cubed
1 tablespoon sesame oil
1 onion, quartered and sliced into rings
1 large garlic clove, chopped
4 stems of pak choy or equivalent
1 sprig of thyme or 1 tablespoon dried thyme
1 teaspoon tabasco sauce (optional)

Directions:

Heat sesame oil in a large pan on a medium high heat before sweating the onions and garlic.

Add the vegetable stock and bring to a boil over a high heat before adding the squash.

Turn down heat and allow to simmer for 25 to 30 minutes.

Soak the mushrooms in the water if not already done, and then press out the liquid and add to the stock into the pot.

Use the mushroom water in the stock for extra taste.

Add the rest of the ingredients except for the greens and allow to simmer for a further 15 minutes or until the squash is tender.

Add in the chopped greens and let them wilt before serving. Serve with the tabasco sauce if you like it spicy.

NUTRITION: Calories: 607   Fat: 44g   Protein: 45g   Total Carbs: 6g Fiber: 3g Net Carbs: 3g

Baked Navy Beans

Prep Time: 15 minutes.   **Cook time:** 8 hours   **Serves:** 4 to 6

Ingredients:
2 cups dried navy beans, soaked in water overnight, drained, and rinsed 6 cups vegetable broth
¼ cup dried cranberries
1 medium sweet onion, diced
½ cup sugarfree ketchup
3 tablespoons olive oil
2 tablespoons maple syrup
2 tablespoons molasses
1 tablespoon apple cider vinegar
1 teaspoon Dijon mustard
1 teaspoon sea salt
½ teaspoon garlic powder

Directions:

In your slow cooker, combine the beans, broth, cranberries, onion, ketchup, olive oil, maple syrup, molasses, vinegar, mustard, salt, and garlic powder.

Cover the cooker and set to low. Cook for 7 to 8 hours and serve.

Cooking tip: it's extremely important to soak your beans before using them in a recipe. It reduces the phytic acid, reduces cooking time, ensures an even cooking experience, and allows your tummy the best (and least painful) experience as it digests them. You can even use the bowl of your slow cooker the night before to soak your beans in cool water with a dash of salt. Make sure it's at room temperature and the beans get at least an 8hour bath. Rinse them well before using, and discard the soaking water.

NUTRITION: Calories 380; Fat 5g; Sodium 1092mg; Carbs 58g; Fiber 15g; Sugars 11g; Protein 20.6g

Honey Mustard Chicken

Prep Time: 10 minutes **Cooking Time:** 35 minutes **Serve:** 4

Ingredients:
1 ½ lbs chicken thighs
½ tsp Italian seasoning
5 garlic cloves, minced
1 ½ tbsp honey
¼ tsp dried parsley
1 ½ tbsp canola oil
1 ½ tbsp Dijon mustard
Pepper
Salt

Directions:
Preheat the oven to 425 F.
Season chicken with pepper and salt and place it into the baking dish.
Mix remaining ingredients, pour over chicken and bake in a preheated oven for 35 minutes.
Serve and enjoy.

NUTRITION: Calories 403 Fat 11 g Carbohydrates 3 g Sugar 7 g Protein 48 g Cholesterol 151 mg

Cheddar & Kale Frittata

Servings: 6

Ingredients:
1/3 c. sliced scallions
¼ teaspoon pepper
1 diced red pepper
¾ c. nonfat milk
1 c. shredded sharp lowfat cheddar cheese
1 teaspoon olive oil
5 oz. baby kale and spinach
12 eggs

Directions:
preheat the oven to 375 0F.
With olive oil, grease a glass casserole dish.
In a bowl, whisk well all ingredients except for cheese.
Pour egg mixture into the o prepared dish and bake for 35 minutes.
Remove from oven and sprinkle cheese on top and broil for 5 minutes.
Remove from the oven and let it sit for 10 minutes.
Cut up and enjoy.

NUTRITION: Calories: 198, Fat:10 g, Carbs:7 g, Protein:17 g, Sugars:1 g, Sodium:209 mg.

Cabbage Soup

Prep Time: 10 minutes. **Cooking time:** 45 minutes. **Servings:** 4

Ingredients:
2 Cup green cabbage
2 Carrots
1 medium onion
½ Cup mushrooms
2 Cup vegetable stock
1 Cup of water
1 tablespoon thyme
1 tablespoon rosemary
Sea salt to taste
Pepper to taste

Directions:

1 Slice all the vegetables and put them in a pot with the vegetable stock.
2 Add water and put it on medium heat for 15–20 minutes. Let it boil, then lower the heat and add the thyme and rosemary and cook for more than 25 minutes.
3 Season the soup with salt and pepper
4 Serve hot.

NUTRITION: Calories: 90 Carbohydrates: 20 g Protein: 5 g Fat: 1 g Sugar: 0 g Fiber: 5 g Sodium: 521 mg

Chicken with Snow Peas and Brown Rice

Prep Time: 10 minutes **Cook time:** 5 minutes **Serves 4**

Ingredients:
1 tablespoon coconut oil
2 cups cooked brown rice
1 cup cooked chicken, cut into ½inch cubes
4 ounces (113 g) snow peas, strings removed
½ cup chicken broth
1 teaspoon salt
½ teaspoon ground ginger
1 teaspoon toasted sesame oil
1 teaspoon coconut aminos
2 scallions, sliced

Directions:

In a large pan over high heat, melt the coconut oil. Add the rice and chicken. Sauté for about 2 minutes. Add the snow peas, chicken broth, salt, and ginger. Cover the pan, reduce the heat to low, and cook for 3 minutes, or until the snow peas turn bright green.
Remove the pan from the heat. Stir in the sesame oil, coconut aminos, and scallions.

NUTRITION: calories: 285 fat: 7g protein: 15g carbs: 39g fiber: 3g sugar: 1g sodium: 705mg

Beef and Mushroom Pasta

Prep Time: 10 minutes **Cooking Time:** 20 minutes **Servings:** 4

Ingredients:

1 tablespoon unsalted butter
1 cup thinly sliced mushrooms
½ onion, finely chopped
8 ounces ground beef
1 teaspoon salt
½ teaspoon dried oregano
¼ teaspoon freshly ground black pepper
2 cups chicken broth or water
8 ounces glutenfree elbow macaroni
¼ cup grated sheep's milk pecorino cheese

Directions :

In a large pot, melt the butter over high heat.
Add the mushrooms and onion and sauté until the softened, about 3 minutes.
Crumble the ground beef into the pot, and add the salt, oregano, and pepper.
Cook the beef until browned on all sides, 3 to 4 minutes total. If desired, drain any extra Fat: that may accumulate in the pot.
Add the broth and macaroni and bring to a boil. Cook, uncovered, until the macaroni is tender, about 8 minutes.
Sprinkle with the cheese and serve.

NUTRITION: Calories: 370Total Fat: 11gTotal Carbohydrates: 44gSugar: 2gFiber: 6g Protein: 23g Sodium: 1168mg

Tabbouleh Salad

Prep Time: 20 minutes **Cooking time:** 15 minutes **Servings:** 4

If you want to lose weight, improve heart health or detox your system, this is the salad for you.

Ingredients:

2 C. water, filtered
1 C. millet, rinsed
⅓ C. extravirgin olive oil
Juice of 1 lemon
1 large garlic clove, crushed
1½ tsp. Himalayan pink salt, divided
2 large tomatoes, rinsed and finely diced
3 scallions, white parts only, rinsed and thinly sliced ½ English cucumber, rinsed and finely diced
¾ C. fresh mint, rinsed and finely chopped
1½ C. fresh parsley, rinsed and finely chopped

Directions:

Boil water over high heat. Add the millet and turn the heat to low.
Cover the pan and cook for 15 minutes.

Remove the pan from the heat and mash the millet with a fork. Let cool with the lid off for 15 minutes. It should be firm, but not crunchy or mushy.

Meanwhile, in a small bowl, whisk the olive oil, lemon juice, garlic, and ½ tsp. of salt. Let sit.

In a large bowl, combine the tomatoes, scallions, cucumber, mint, and parsley. Add the cooled millet. Pour the dressing over and mix well. Taste and season with the remaining 1 tsp. of salt, as needed.

NUTRITION: Calories: 3937 kcal Total Fat: 258 g Total Carbohydrates: 48 g Fiber: 88 g Sugar: 5 g Protein: 6 g

White Bean Chicken with Winter Green Vegetables

Servings: 8 **Cooking Time:** 45 Minutes

Ingredients:
4 Garlic cloves
1tablespoon Olive oil
3 medium parsnips
1kg Small cubes of chicken
1 Teaspoon cumin powder
2 Leaks & 1 Green part
2 Carrots (cut into cubes)
1 ¼ White kidney beans (overnight soaked)
½ Teaspoon dried oregano
2 Teaspoon Kosher salt Cilantro leaves
1 1/2tablespoon Ground ancho chilies

Directions:
Cook garlic, leeks, chicken, and olive oil in a large pot on a medium flame for 5
minutes.
Now add carrots and parsnips, and after stirring for 2 minutes, add all seasoning ingredients.
Stir until the fragrant starts coming from it.
Now add beans and 5 cups of water in the pot.
Bring it to a boil and reduce the flame.
Allow it to simmer almost for 30 minutes and garnish with parsley and cilantro leaves.

NUTRITION: Calories 263 Carbs: 24g Fat: 7g Protein: 26g

Rosemary and Garlic Sweet Potatoes

Prep Time: 10 Minutes **Cooking Time:** 15 Minutes **Servings:** 4

Ingredients:
2 tablespoons extravirgin olive oil
2 sweet potatoes (skin left on), cut into ½inch cubes 1 tablespoon chopped fresh rosemary leaves
½ teaspoon of sea salt
3 garlic cloves, minced
¼ teaspoon freshly ground black pepper

Directions:
In a big nonstick skillet over mediumhigh heat, heat the olive oil until it shimmers.

Supply the sweet potatoes, rosemary, and salt. Cook for 10 to a quarterhour, stirring occasionally until the sweet potatoes start to brown.
Put the garlic and pepper. Cook for 30 seconds, stirring constantly.

NUTRITION: Calories: 199Kcal Proteins: 2g Carbohydrates: 33g Fat: 7g

Breakfast Burgers with Avocado Buns

Prep Time: 10 minutes **Cooking time:** 5 minutes **Servings:** 1

Ingredients:
1 ripe avocado
1 egg, pastureraised
1 red onion slice
1 tomato slice
1 lettuce leaf
Sesame seed for garnish
salt to taste

Directions:
Peel the avocado and remove the seed. Slice the avocado into half. This will serve as the bun. Set aside.
Grease a skillet over medium flame and fry the egg sunny side up for 5
minutes or until set.
Assemble the breakfast burger by placing on top of one avocado half with the egg, red onion, tomato, and lettuce leaf. Top with the remaining avocado bun.
Garnish with sesame seeds on top and season with salt to taste.

NUTRITION: Calories 458, Total Fat 39g, Saturated Fat 4g, Total Carbs 20g, Net Carbs 6g, Protein 13g, Sugar: 8g, Fiber: 14g, Sodium: 118mg, Potassium 1184mg

Shrimp Pasta with Lemon and Garlic

Prep Time: 10 Minutes **Cooking Time:** 15 Minutes **Servings:** 3

Ingredients:
6 ounces (170 g) bean pasta
1 head broccoli, chopped into florets
3 tablespoons olive oil, divided
¾ pound (340 g) large shrimp, peeled and deveined 2 garlic cloves, minced
½ teaspoon salt
½ teaspoon freshly ground black pepper
Juice of 1 lemon
3 cups baby spinach

Directions:
Bring a large pot of water to a boil over high heat. Cook the pasta according to package instructions (usually 8 to 10 minutes). Add the broccoli for the final 2 minutes. Drain the pasta and broccoli and set them aside in the same pot they were cooked in.
Meanwhile, in a large skillet, heat 2 tablespoons of olive oil over medium heat. Add the shrimp and cook without turning for 5 minutes.
Add the garlic, then flip the shrimp to cook on the other side for 3 to 4

minutes, or until cooked through completely and pink in hue. Sprinkle the shrimp with the salt and pepper, add the lemon juice, and cook for 1
minute more.

Toss the pasta and broccoli with the remaining 1 tablespoon of olive oil.

Place 1 cup of baby spinach into each of 3 medium containers. Divide the broccoli and pasta into 3 large containers. Top each pasta container with a portion of shrimp.

NUTRITION: Calories: 436Kcal Proteins: 45g Carbohydrates: 32g Fat: 15g

Sweet Potato Chips

Prep Time: 20 minutes **Cooking Time:** 2 hours **Servings:** 6

Ingredients:

3 Tablespoons extravirgin olive oil
1 teaspoon of sea salt
2 larges thinly sliced sweet potatoes

Directions:

Power on the oven and heat it to 250°F. Place the rack in the center of the oven.

Take a large bowl and drop in the sweet potatoes' slices along with olive oil. Arrange the slices individually on 2 baking sheets—dust with the sea salt.

Lay the sheets inside the preheated oven and bake for about two hours; make sure to rotate the pans and flip the chips after 45 – 60 minutes.

As soon as the chips turn light brown and attain the crispiness, take them off the oven. Some may be a bit mushy, but they will again turn crisp as they begin to cool.

Let the chips cool for about ten minutes before serving. Serve straight away. The chips will again turn mushy after a few hours.

NUTRITION: Carbohydrate: 43g Protein: 7g Total Fat: 11g Calories: 268 Cholesterol: 0.0mg Fiber: 5g Sodium: 483mg

Strawberry Granita

Prep Time: 20 minutes   **Cook time:** 0 minutes   **Servings:** 8

Ingredients:

4 cups hot water
2 medium pitted dates
2 white tea bags (decaffeinated if children under twelve years old are served) 2 cups strawberries

Directions:

Place hot water in a suitable bowl or pitcher. Add dates and tea bags. Steep 20 minutes.
Remove tea bags. Cool.
Pour cooled tea and dates into blender. Add strawberries. Blend until smooth.
Pour blended mixture into a large glass casserole dish and place in freezer for almost 2 hours. (if frozen for much longer than that, it becomes harder to scrape.)
Remove from freezer and scrape thoroughly with a fork into small ice crystals. If bottom layers are not yet frozen enough to scrape, return to freezer for another hour and repeat scraping.
Serve in parfait cups.

NUTRITION: Calories 17; Fat 0.1g; Sodium 4mg; Carbs 3g; Fiber 0.9g; Sugars 1g; Protein 0.3g

Ruby Pears Delight

Prep Time: 10 minutes Cooking time: 10 minutes Servings: 4

Rich in antioxidants, dietary fiber and essential vitamins, pears are a good source of compounds to manage or curb inflammatory diseases.

Ingredients:
4 pears
26 oz. grape juice
11 oz. currant jelly
4 garlic cloves
Juice and zest of 1 lemon
4 peppercorns
2 rosemary springs
½ vanilla bean

Directions:
Pour the jelly and grape juice in your instant pot and mix with lemon zest and juice .
Dip each pear into the mix and wrap them in a clean piece of tinfoil, and place them orderly in the steamer basket of your instant pot.
Combine peppercorns, rosemary, garlic cloves, and vanilla bean to the juice mixture.
Seal the lid and cook at high for 10 minutes.
Release the pressure quickly, and carefully open the lid; bring out the pears, remove wrappers and arrange them on plates. Serve when cold with toppings of cooking juice.

NUTRITION: Calories: 4035 kcal Fat: 0.51 g Fiber: 98 g Carbs: 100.54 g Protein: 49 g

Pasta Primavera

Prep Time: 10 minutes **Cooking Time:** 20 minutes **Servings:** 4

Ingredients :
2 tablespoons unsalted butter
1 leek, white part only, thinly sliced
1 pound pencilthin asparagus, trimmed of woody ends and cut into ½
inch pieces
1 cup frozen green peas, thawed
1 teaspoon salt
¼ teaspoon freshly ground black pepper
½ cup white wine
2 cups vegetable broth or water
8 ounces glutenfree ziti
½ cup crumbled goat cheese cheese
2 tablespoons finely chopped fresh basil
Directions :
In a large pot, melt the butter over high heat.
Add the leek, asparagus, peas, salt, and pepper and sauté until softened, 1 to 2 minutes.
Add the wine and cook until it is reduced by half, 3 to 5 minutes.

Add the broth and ziti and bring to a boil. Cook, uncovered, until the ziti is tender, 10 to 12 minutes.
Add the cheese and stir until it melts into the ziti.
Sprinkle with the basil and serve.

NUTRITION: Calories: 409Total Fat: 11gTotal Carbohydrates: 55gSugar: 7gFiber: 10g Protein:17g
Sodium: 1066mg

Tricky Cheesy Yellow Sauce

Servings: 2 **Cooking Time:** 0 Minutes

Ingredients:

1½ cups steamed, mashed cauliflower florets and hot ½ cup coconut milk, fullfat
½ cup nutritional yeast
1 tablespoon unsalted butter, ghee, or lard 1½ teaspoons coconut vinegar
1 teaspoon Himalayan salt, fine
1 teaspoon garlic powder

Directions:

Place all of the ingredients in a blender. Cover and blend on low, slowly bringing the speed up to high.
Continue to blend until the sauce is completely smooth. Taste for seasoning and add a little more salt
and/or garlic powder if you like.
Store in an airtight container in the refrigerator for up to a week.
Warm in a saucepan on the stovetop over medium heat and stir occasionally.

NUTRITION: Calories: 185 ;Fat: 11g ;Protein: 11g;Carbs: 15g .

Fresh Tuna Steak and Fennel Salad

Prep Time: 15 minutes   **Cook time:** 25 minutes   **Serves** 4

Ingredients:

2 (1 inch) tuna steaks
2 tablespoons olive oil, 1 tablespoon olive oil for brushing 1 teaspoon crushed black peppercorns
1 teaspoon crushed fennel seeds
1 fennel bulb, trimmed and sliced
½ cup water
1 lemon, juiced
1 teaspoon fresh parsley, chopped

Directions:

Coat the fish with oil and then season with peppercorns and fennel seeds.
Heat the oil on a medium heat and sauté the fennel bulb slices for 5
minutes or until light brown. Add the water to the pan and cook for 10
minutes until fennel is tender. Stir in the lemon juice and lower heat to a simmer. Meanwhile, heat
another skillet and sauté the tuna steaks for about 2 to 3 minutes each side for mediumrare. (Add 1
minute each side for medium and 2 minutes each side for medium well). Serve the fennel mix with the
tuna steaks on top and garnish with the fresh parsley.

NUTRITION: Calories: 288   fat: 9g   protein: 44g   carbs: 6g   fiber: 2g   sugar: 3g   sodium: 105mg

Healthy Red Cabbage

Prep Time: 10 minutes **Cooking Time:** 20 minutes **Serve:** 4

Ingredients:
1 red cabbage head, sliced
3 tbsp canola oil
2 tbsp parsley, chopped
½ cup balsamic vinegar
Pepper
Salt

Directions:
Heat oil in a pan over mediumhigh heat
Add cabbage to the pan and sauté for 5 minutes.
Add vinegar, pepper, and salt and sauté for 15 minutes or until cabbage is cooked.
Garnish with parsley and serve.
4
NUTRITION: Calories 113 Fat 2 g Carbohydrates 7 g Sugar 9 g Protein 3 g Cholesterol 0 Mg

Easy Chicken and Broccoli

Prep Time: 10 minutes.   **Cook time:** 7 minutes.   **Serves:** 4

Ingredients:
3 tablespoons extravirgin olive oil
1½ pounds skinless chicken breasts, boneless, diced 1½ cups broccoli florets, or chopped broccoli stems ½ onion, chopped
½ teaspoon sea salt
⅛ teaspoon black pepper, freshly ground
3 garlic cloves, minced
2 cups cooked brown rice

Directions:
Cut the chicken breasts into bitesize pieces.
In a suitable skillet over mediumhigh heat, heat the olive oil until it shimmers.
Add the chicken, broccoli, onion, salt, and pepper. Cook for almost 7
minutes, while stirring occasionally, until the chicken is cooked.
Add the garlic. Cook for almost 30 seconds, while stirring constantly.
Toss with the brown rice to serve.

NUTRITION: Calories 389; Fat 19g; Sodium 198mg; Carbs 33g; Fiber 2g; Sugars 0.6g; Protein 28g

Sweet Potato and Butternut Squash Curry

Prep Time: 15 minutes   **Cook time:** 15 minutes   Serves 4 to 6

Ingredients:
1 tablespoon coconut oil
1 onion, chopped
1 large sweet potato, peeled and cut into ½inch cubes 2 cups (½inch) butternut squash cubes
2 garlic cloves, sliced

2 cups nosaltadded vegetable broth
1 (15ounce / 383g) can coconut milk
2 teaspoons curry powder
1 teaspoon sea salt
2 tablespoons chopped fresh cilantro

Directions:

Heat the coconut oil in a Dutch oven over high heat.
Add the onion and sauté for about 3 minutes until softened.
Stir in the sweet potato, butternut squash, and garlic and sauté for 3
minutes more.
Add the vegetable broth, coconut milk, curry powder, and salt to the vegetables, and bring to a boil.
Reduce the heat and bring to a simmer and continue cooking for about 5
minutes, or until the vegetables are forktender.
Sprinkle the cilantro on top for garnish and serve.

NUTRITION: calories: 122   fat: 5g   protein: 2g   carbs: 20g   fiber: 3g   sugar: 4g   sodium: 671mg

Romesco Sauce with Vegetables and Sheet Pan Chicken

Prep Time: 26minutes   **Total time:** 56minutes   **Yield:** 4servings

Ingredients:
2 cubed Yukon gold potatoes
6 tbsps. olive oil
1 tsp. ground black pepper
½ tsp. salt
4 chicken thighs, bonein, and skinless
4 c. broccoli florets
1(7 oz.) jarred pepper, roasted ¼ c. slivered almonds
1 crushed garlic clove
1 tsp. paprika
½ tsp. ground cumin
¼ tsp. red pepper,
crushed
2 tbsps. fresh cilantro, chopped

Directions:

Preheat your oven to attain 450°F. Add the 1/8 tbsp. salt, ¼ tbsp. black pepper, 1 tbsp. oil, and potatoes in a bowl and toss to combine. Transfer the potatoes to one side of a rimmed baking sheet. Add the ¼ tsp. pepper, chicken, 1 tbsp. oil, and 1/8 tbsp. salt into the same bowl and toss to coat.
Transfer the chicken to the other side of the baking sheet. Roast the chicken and potatoes for 10minutes. Meanwhile, add the broccoli, 2 tbsps. oil, ¼
tbsp. pepper, and 1/8 tbsp. salt inside a different bowl then tosses to mix. Add broccoli mixture to the potato side of your baking sheet and stir to mix.
Roast the broccoli for 15minutes. Meanwhile, add the roasted pepper, paprika, red pepper, cumin, almonds, ¼ tbsp. pepper, 2 tbsps. oil,1/8 tbsp.

garlic and salt inside a food processor and process until a smooth consistency is achieved. Transfer the vegetables and chicken to a serving platter and sprinkle with the cilantro. Serve with roasted pepper sauce.

NUTRITION: Calories 499 Total fat 27g Carbs 30g Protein 33g

Zuppa Toscana

Prep Time: 15 minutes or fewer **Cooking Time**: 5 to 6 hours on low **Servings:** 46

Ingredients:
4 cups vegetable broth
2 cups chopped deribbed kale
2 small sweet potatoes, peeled and diced
1 medium zucchini, diced
1 (15ounce) can cannellini beans, rinsed and drained well 1 celery stalk, diced
1 carrot, diced
1 small onion, diced
½ teaspoon garlic powder
½ teaspoon sea salt
¼ teaspoon red pepper flakes
Freshly ground black pepper

Directions:
In your slow cooker, combine the broth, kale, sweet potatoes, zucchini, beans, celery, carrot, onion, garlic powder, salt, and red pepper flakes, and season with black pepper.
Cover the cooker and set to low. Cook for 5 to 6 hours and serve.

NUTRITION: Calories: 209Total Fat: 1gTotal Carbs: 43gSugar: 9gFiber: 10g Protein: 8g Sodium: 871mg

Healthy Broccoli Soup

Prep Time: 10 minutes **Cooking Time:** 3 hours **Serve:** 6

Ingredients:
8 cups broccoli florets
2 tbsp olive oil
6 cups vegetable stock
1 tbsp olive oil
2 tbsp ginger, chopped
4 cups leeks, chopped
1 tsp turmeric
1/8 tsp pepper
1 tsp salt

Directions:
Add broccoli and remaining ingredients into the crockpot and stir well.
Cover and cook on low for 3 hours.
Puree the soup using a blender until smooth. Season with pepper and salt.
Serve and enjoy.
NUTRITION: Calories 151 Fat 8 g Carbohydrates 19 g Sugar 1 g Protein 9 g cholesterol 0 mg

Shrimp and Mango Mix

Prep Time: 10 minutes **Cooking Time:** 0 minutes **Servings:** 5

Ingredients:

2 tablespoons Dijon mustard
3 tablespoons white wine vinegar
6 tablespoons avocado mayonnaise
4 cucumbers, peeled and cubed
1 mango, peeled and cubed
3 tablespoons chopped dill
1 pound shrimp, cooked, peeled and deveined
A pinch of salt and black pepper

Directions:

1. In a salad bowl, mix the cucumbers with the mango, shrimp, dill, salt and pepper and toss. Add the mustard, vinegar and mayonnaise and mix well then serve.

NUTRITION: Calories: 174Fat: 3Fiber: 2Carbs: 4

LemonHerb Tilapia

Prep Time: 15 minutes **Cooking Time:** 20 minutes **Servings:** 1

Ingredients:

2 6 oz. tilapia fillets
1 tsp dried tarragon
2 whole lemons
1 tbsp olive oil
1 tsp dried thyme
1 tsp kosher salt
1/2 tsp black pepper

Directions:

Preheat the oven to 350°F.
Combine the tarragon, thyme, kosher salt, and pepper in a small mixing bowl.
Set aside one of the lemons in thin slices (with skin on), carefully removing any seeds.
Cut the remaining lemon in halves and pour the juice over the tilapia filets, covering them evenly.
Season the tilapia on both sides with the dry herb seasoning combination.
In an ovensafe skillet over mediumhigh heat, heat the olive oil.
Cook the tilapia in the heated skillet for 35 minutes, or until golden brown. Flip the fish over and pour in more lemon juice from the half lemon. Place the lemon slices flat on the skillet and fish, then bake for 35 minutes, or until the fish is cooked through and flaky.
 Garnish the fish with caramelized lemon slices.

GingerBroccoli Salad

Prep Time: 20 minutes **Cooking Time:** 0 minutes **Servings:** 3

Ingredients

¼ tsp sea salt

¼ tsp ground cinnamon
½ tsp ground turmeric
¾ tsp ground ginger
½ tbsp extra virgin olive oil
½ tbsp apple cider vinegar
2 tbsp chopped green onion
1/3 cup coconut cream
½ cup carrots, shredded
1 small head of broccoli, chopped

Directions
In a large salad bowl, mix well salt, cinnamon, turmeric, ginger, olive oil, and vinegar.
Add remaining Ingredients, tossing well to coat.
Pop in the ref for at least 30 to 60 minutes before serving.

NUTRITION: Calories: 113Total Fat: 10gSaturated Fat: 2gTotal Carbs: 5gNet Carbs: 3g Protein: 2gSugar: 1gFiber: 2g Sodium: 233mgPotassium: 198mg

Oregano Dressing on Salad Greens
Prep Time: 15 minutes **Cooking Time:** 0 minutes **Servings:** 4

Ingredients
1/3 cup chopped red onion
¾ cup crumbled soft fresh goat cheese
1 ½ cups diced celery
1 ½ large red bell peppers, diced
4 cups baby spinach leaves, coarsely chopped
1 tbsp chopped fresh oregano
2 tbsp fresh lemon juice
2 tbsp extra virgin olive oil

Directions:
In a large salad bowl, mix oregano, lemon juice and oil.
Add pepper and salt to taste.
Mix in red onion, goat cheese, celery, bell peppers and spinach.
Toss to coat well, serve and enjoy.

NUTRITION: Calories: 91Total Fat: 4gSaturated Fat: 0gTotal Carbs: 11gNet Carbs: 5g Protein: 6gSugar: 3gFiber: 6g Sodium: 207mgPotassium: 720mg

ChocolateCoated Banana
Time: 20 minutes **Serving Size:** 12 **Prep Time:** 20 minutes **Cook Time:** o minutes
This one is easy and treats you to your favorite popsicle dip even on this diet, because all the ingredients used possess curative powers that help control chronic inflammation.
Ingredients:
1 cup almonds rubbed in chili powder, coarsely chopped
1 cup pistachios, coarsely chopped
1 cup hazelnuts, coarsely chopped
3 cups dark chocolate chips

1 tbsp white coconut oil
6 large bananas
Dried and chopped berries of your choice

Directions:
Peel, cut bananas in half and insert a popsicle stick to the end that is cut. Place the fruits on a lined tray and freeze for 20 minutes.

Next, melt the chocolate with the oil over a low flame, and stir until it becomes smooth. Then pour it into a bowl large enough to dip the bananas.

Take out the bananas and line up your chocolate and chopped nuts, as well as the fruit.

Take a large piece of parchment paper on which you will arrange the bowls with the berries, nuts and chocolate.

Now, dip a banana in the chocolate mix and sprinkle it with the nuts, and if you like, the berries too. Alternate between types of nuts and berries until you have coated all 12 halves.

Place each coated banana back on the tray, and freeze for about 10–20 minutes before enjoying your treat.

NUTRITION: Calories 210 Carbs 25 g Fat 14 g Protein 14 g Fiber 14 g

Refreshing Apple Smoothie

Prep Time: 5 minutes **Cooking Time:** 5 minutes **Serve:** 1

Ingredients:
1 medium apple, chopped
¼ tsp ground ginger
¼ tsp cinnamon
1 scoop vanilla protein powder
¾ cup spinach
1 ½ cups unsweetened almond milk

Directions:
Add chopped apple and remaining ingredients into the blender and blend until smooth and creamy. Serve immediately and enjoy.

NUTRITION: Calories 184 Fat 5 g Carbohydrates 35 g Sugar 23 g Protein 2 g Cholesterol 0 mg

Delicious Mango Smoothie

Prep Time: 5 minutes **Cooking Time:** 5 minutes **Serve:** 1

Ingredients:
1 cup mango chunks
¼ tsp turmeric
1 tsp vanilla
1 banana
½ cup orange juice
1 scoop vanilla protein powder
1 cup unsweetened almond milk

Directions:

Add mango chunks and remaining ingredients into the blender and blend until smooth and creamy. Serve immediately and enjoy.

NUTRITION: Calories 314 Fat 4 g Carbohydrates 67 g Sugar 47 g Protein 4 g Cholesterol 0 mg

Healthy Spinach Smoothie

Prep Time: 5 minutes **Cooking Time:** 5 minutes **Serve:** 2

Ingredients:
1 1/2 cups fresh spinach
½ cup ice
1 ½ cups cashew milk
1 pear, cored & diced
1/4 banana
½ cup water

Directions:
Add pear and remaining ingredients into the blender and blend until smooth and creamy. Serve immediately and enjoy.

NUTRITION: Calories 77 Fat 7 g Carbohydrates 15 g Sugar 8 g Protein 1 g Cholesterol 0 mg

Full Coconut Cake

Prep Time: 5minutes **Total time:** 50minutes **Yield:** 4servings

Ingredients:
3 eggs, yolks, and whites
¾ c. Coconut Flour
separated
½ tsp. Coconut Extract
1 ½ c. warm Coconut Milk
½ c. Coconut Sugar
2 tbsp. melted Coconut Oil
1 c. Water

Directions:
Beat the whites until soft form peaks. Beat in the eggyolks along with the coconut sugar. Whisk in coconut extract and coconut oil. Gently fold in the coconut flour.
Line a baking dish and pour the batter inside. Cover with aluminum foil.
Pour the water inside your Instant Pot. Put the container in the pressure cooker. Close the lid and cook for 45minutes in MANUAL mode. Do a quick pressure release. Serve and enjoy.

NUTRITION: Calories 350, Carbohydrates 47 g, Fiber 5 g, Fat 11 g, Protein 5 g

Blueberry Crisp

Prep Time: 15 minutes **Cook time:** 20 minutes **Serves** 4

Ingredients:
½ cup coconut oil, melted, plus additional for brushing 1 quart fresh blueberries
¼ cup maple syrup

Juice of ½ lemon
2 teaspoons lemon zest
1 cup glutenfree rolled oats
½ teaspoon ground cinnamon
½ cup chopped pecans
Pinch salt

Directions:
 Preheat the oven to 350ºF (180ºC). Brush a shallow baking dish with melted coconut oil. Stir together the blueberries, maple syrup, lemon juice, and lemon zest in the dish. In a small bowl, combine the oats, ½ cup of melted coconut oil, cinnamon, pecans, and salt. Mix the ingredients well to evenly distribute the coconut oil. Sprinkle the oat mixture over the berries.
Place the dish in the preheated oven and bake for 20 minutes, or until the oats are lightly browned.

NUTRITION: Calories: 497   fat: 33g   protein: 5g   carbs: 51g   fiber: 7g   sugar: 26g   sodium: 42mg

Vanilla Coconut Cake

Prep Time: 15 minutes   **Cook time:** 45 minutes   **Serves** 8

Ingredients:
½ cup coconut oil, melted, plus more for greasing the baking dish 2 cups egg whites (about 12), at room temperature Pinch sea salt
1 cup unsweetened almond milk
6 tablespoons raw honey
2 teaspoons pure vanilla extract
1 cup coconut flour
½ cup shredded unsweetened coconut
2 teaspoons baking powder

Directions:
 Preheat the oven to 350ºF (180ºC).
 Lightly grease a baking dish with coconut oil and set it aside.
 In a large bowl, beat the egg whites and sea salt with an electric mixer until soft peaks form. Set them aside.
 In another large bowl, whisk the almond milk, honey, remaining ½ cup of coconut oil, and the vanilla.
 Whisk in the coconut flour, coconut, and baking powder until well combined.
 Fold the beaten egg whites into the batter, keeping as much volume as possible, until just blended. Spoon the batter into the prepared dish and smooth the top.
 Bake the cake for about 45 minutes, or until cooked through and lightly browned.
 Cool the cake completely on a wire rack.
 Serve with fresh fruit, if desired.

NUTRITION: Calories: 237   fat: 17g   protein: 7g   carbs: 16g   fiber: 1g   sugar: 15g   sodium: 136mg

Chocolate Bananas

Prep Time: 5 Minutes **Cooking Time:** 15 Minutes **Servings:** 4

Ingredients:
3 Bananas, large & cut into thirds

12 oz. Dark Chocolate
1 tbsp. Coconut Oil

Directions:
To begin with, melt the chocolate and coconut oil in a double boiler for 3 to 4 minutes or until you get a smooth and glossy mixture.
Next, keep the popsicles into the end of each of the banana by inserting it.
After that, immerse the chocolate into the warm chocolate mixture.
Shake off the excess chocolate and place them on parchment paper.
Sprinkle with the topping of your choice.
Finally, place them in the freezer for a few hours or until set.

NUTRITION: Calories: 427Kcal Protein:9g Carbohydrates: 80g Fat: 16g

Sweet Porridge Dessert

Prep Time: 10 minutes **Cooking Time:** 30 minutes **Servings:** 4

Ingredients
For the porridge:
1 ½ cups coconut milk
½ cup steel cut oats
½ cup water
2 black tea bags
1 teaspoon vanilla extract
2 tablespoons raw honey
For the acai berry ripple:
2 tablespoons acai powder
1 cup berries
1 tablespoon maple syrup
For the pistachio cream:
¼ cup pistachios, roasted
½ cup coconut milk

Directions
Put ½ cup water in a pot and heat up over medium heat. Add oats, vanilla extract, tea bags and 1 and ½ cups coconut milk. Stir well, bring to a simmer, cover and cook for 30 minutes. Discard tea bags then add honey, stir well and take off heat. In a blender, puree 1 cup berries with acai powder and maple syrup then transfer to a bowl. In the same blender, add ½ cup coconut milk and pistachios and puree. Divide oats into bowls, add acai ripple and top with pistachios cream then serve.
Enjoy!

NUTRITION: Calories: 140Fat: 4Fiber: 2Carbs: 6Protein: 5

Mini Spinach Muffins

Servings: 12 Muffins **Cooking Time:** 15 Minutes

Ingredients:
2 cups packed spinach
¼ cup raw honey

1 teaspoon vanilla extract
3 tablespoons extravirgin olive oil
2 eggs
1 cup almond flour
1 cup oat flour
1 teaspoon baking soda
2 teaspoons baking powder
½ teaspoon salt
Pinch freshly ground black pepper

Directions:

Preheat the oven to 350ºF (180ºC). Line a 12cup muffin pan with paper muffin cups.

Put the spinach, honey, vanilla, and olive oil in a food processor, then break the eggs into it. Pulse to mix well until creamy and smooth.

Combine the flours, baking soda, baking powder, salt, and black pepper in a large bowl. Stir to mix well.

Make a well in the center of the flour mixture, then pour the spinach mixture into the well. Stir to mix well.

Divide the batter into muffin cups, then arrange the muffin pan in the preheated oven and bake for 15 minutes or until a toothpick inserted in the center comes out clean.

Remove the pan from the oven. Allow to cool for 10 minutes, then serve immediately.

NUTRITION: calories: 107; fat: 8g ; protein: 2g ; carbs: 19g ; fiber: 0g ; sugar: 5g ; sodium: 216mg

Lemon Ginger Broccoli And Carrots

Servings: 6 **Cooking Time**: 5 Minutes

Ingredients:
1 tablespoon avocado oil
1" fresh ginger, peeled and thinly sliced
1 clove garlic, minced
2 broccoli crowns, florets
2 large carrots, sliced
½ teaspoon kosher salt Juice from
½ large lemon
¼ cup of water

Directions:

Put the oil to the inner pot. Heatup within 2 minutes.

Add the ginger and garlic and sauté 1 minute. Add the broccoli, carrots, and salt and stir to combine. Turn off.

Add the lemon juice and water and use a wooden spoon to scrape up any brown bits—Cook within 2 minutes.

Serve immediately.

NUTRITION: Calories 67 Fat: 2g Protein: 3g Sodium: 245mg Fiber: 3g Carbohydrates: 10g Sugar: 3g

A simple pudding sweetened with peanut butter

Prep Time: 10 minutes **Cooking time:** 0 minutes **Servings:** 4

Ingredients
⅛ tsp. nutmeg, ground
½ C. peanuts, raw and unsalted
⅛ tsp. salt, iodized
⅓ C. pumpkin puree
¼ tsp. cinnamon, ground
⅛ C. pure maple syrup
¼ C. almond milk, unsweetened
½ tbsp. coconut oil, melted
⅛ cloves, ground

Directions:
Pulse nutmeg, peanuts, salt, pumpkin puree, cinnamon, maple syrup, almond milk, coconut oil, and cloves for approximately 3
minutes.
Make sure all ingredients are incorporated. Divide equally into individual glasses or a dish.
Serve immediately and enjoy!

NUTRITION: Calories: 1518 kcal Fat: 89 g Fiber: 36 g Carbs: 153 g Protein: 99 g 29

Rice Pudding

Prep Time: 5 minutes **Cooking time:** 20 minutes **Servings:** 4

Rice is fiber packed with macronutrients good for the body.
Ingredients
4 ⅓ C. almond milk, unsweetened
3½ oz. brown rice
2 tbsp. pure maple syrup, separated

Directions:
Empty milk in a saucepan on the highest heat setting. As it starts to bubble, turn heat to medium/low, then transfer the rice into the pot.
Toss to cover the rice completely. Toss frequently for 20 minutes or until it reaches the desired thickness.
Transfer to serving dishes and drizzle each with ½ tbsp. maple syrup.

NUTRITION: per serving Calories: 1514 kcal Fat: 92 g Fiber: 0.89 g Carbs: 216 g Protein: 55 g

Quick Fish Bowl

Prep Time: 11minutes **Total time:** 26minutes **Yield:** 2servings

Ingredients:
2 tilapia fillets
1 tbsp. olive oil
1 avocado
1 tbsp. ghee butter

1 tbsp. cumin powder
1 tbsp. paprika
2 c. coleslaw cabbage, chopped
1 tbsp. salsa sauce
Himalayan rock salt, to taste
Black pepper to taste

Directions:
Heat the oven to 424F. Using a foil, line a baking sheet. Puree the avocado.
Using olive oil, brush the tilapia fillets and season with spices and salt.
Grease with the ghee butter and put the fish onto the baking sheet.
Let it bake for 15minutes, then remove it from the heat. Allow it to cool for 5minutes. Mix and gently toss the salsa sauce and the coleslaw cabbage in a bowl. Add the mashed avocado, season with pepper and salt Cut the fish and add to the bowl. Bake for 1415minutes. Serve hot.

NUTRITION: Carbs: 5,2 g Fat: 24,5 g Protein: 16,1 g

Quinoa Salmon Bowl

Prep Time: 15 minutes **Cook time:** 0 minutes **Serves** 4

Ingredients:
4 cups cooked quinoa
1 pound (454 g) cooked salmon, flaked
3 cups arugula
6 radishes, thinly sliced
1 zucchini, sliced into half moons
3 scallions, minced
½ cup almond oil
1 tablespoon apple cider vinegar
1 teaspoon Sriracha or other hot sauce (or more if you like it spicy) 1 teaspoon salt
½ cup toasted slivered almonds (optional)

Directions:
 Combine the quinoa, salmon, arugula, radishes, zucchini, and scallions in a large bowl. Add the almond oil, vinegar, Sriracha, and salt and mix well.
Divide the mixture among four serving bowls, garnish with the toasted almonds (if using), and serve.

NUTRITION: Calories: 790   fat: 52g   protein: 37g   carbs: 45g   fiber: 8g   sugar: 4g   sodium: 680mg

ManhattanStyle Salmon Chowder

Prep Time: 10 minutes **Cook time:** 15 minutes **Serves** 4

Ingredients:
¼ cup extravirgin olive oil
1 red bell pepper, chopped
1 pound (454 g) skinless salmon, pin bones removed, and chopped into ½
inch pieces
2 (28 ounces / 794 g) cans crushed tomatoes, 1 drained and 1 undrained 6 cups nosaltadded chicken broth

2 cups diced sweet potatoes
1 teaspoon onion powder
½ teaspoon sea salt
¼ teaspoon freshly ground black pepper

Directions:
 In a large pot over mediumhigh heat, heat the olive oil until it shimmers.
 Add the red bell pepper and salmon. Cook for about 5 minutes, stirring occasionally, until the fish is opaque and the bell pepper is soft. Stir in the tomatoes, chicken broth, sweet potatoes, onion powder, salt, and pepper.
Bring to a simmer and reduce the heat to medium. Cook for about 10
minutes, stirring occasionally, until the sweet potatoes are soft.

NUTRITION: Calories: 570   fat: 39g   protein: 41g   carbs: 55g   fiber: 16g   sugar: 24g   sodium: 600mg

Savory Brown Rice with Shrimp and Avocado

Time: 60 minutes **Serving Size:** 8 portions   **Prep Time**: 20 minutes **Cook Time**: 40 minutes
This comforting rice dish comes very close to paella, but is not as complicated. You can make the rice on its own to be enjoyed with your favorite topping. I have chosen a topping of shrimp and avocado in this recipe, but it works well with any combination of meat or seafood.
Besides, I find that cooking up an extra batch of this dish and freezing it comes in handy for days I'm running late, because the rice can be easily popped in a Dutch oven or multicooker to reheat while you relax.

Ingredients:
1 mediumsize onion, chopped
1 mediumsize red pepper, chopped
1 cup portobello mushrooms, sliced — these have a nice firm texture and soak up loads of flavor
2 tbsp olive oil
2 cups longgrain brown rice
I use a good organic longgrain brown rice that's free from gluten and additives, thus increasing its nutritional value
A note on the rice; I generally wash the rice twice over, draining out the starch. Prepare your rice thus, and have it ready for cooking
3 cloves of garlic, minced
1 tsp ginger, minced
1 tsp turmeric
2 tsp chili powder
1 tsp salt
1 tsp pepper
1 ½ cup avocado, sliced
2 lbs shrimp, shelled and deveined
4 cups vegetable stock
Half a lime wedge

Directions:

Use a large stockpot or Dutch oven for this recipe. On mediumhigh heat, add a tablespoon of oil, then onion, half the garlic and ginger. Stir, while allowing them to cook for about 2–3 minutes.

Once you see the onions are releasing their oil, stir in the washed rice, and add the turmeric. Let the ingredients mix well for 2–3 minutes.

Add the stock, and give the rice a good stir. You can now add the salt as desired. Cover and cook for 25–30 minutes.

While the rice cooks, wash and prepare your shrimp and red pepper. Heat the remaining oil in a skillet on mediumhigh heat and then add the shrimp, and season with salt. Then add the garlic and the chili powder.

Keep in mind that shrimp cook fast, and you want them firm and juicy, so be sure not to overcook them. Keep cooking the shrimp for 4–5 minutes, and when they start to turn pink, add the chopped red pepper, and cook while mixing the ingredients for another 2–3 minutes.

Now, check your rice. Once it has absorbed the stock, it should be ready. Fluff it up with a fork, and turn off the heat. Keep the lid open to release steam.

Once the shrimp are done, slice your avocado. Dish your rice into a serving platter and arrange the avocado slices around the rim, then spoon the shrimp into the middle section. Now, give a generous squeeze of lime over the shrimp and avocado. You can season the avocado with salt and pepper if you desire, although the rice and shrimp will add plenty of flavors.

NUTRITION: Calories 331 Carbs 44 g Fat 7 g Protein24 g Fiber 4 g

Brisket With Blue Cheese

Servings: 6 **Cooking Time:** 8 Hrs. 10 Minutes

Ingredients:
1 cup of water
1/2 tablespoon garlic paste
1/4 cup soy sauce
1 ½ lb. corned beef brisket
1/3 teaspoon ground coriander
1/4 teaspoon cloves, ground
1 tablespoon olive oil
1 shallot, chopped
2 oz. blue cheese, crumbled
Cooking spray

Directions:
Place a pan over moderate heat and add oil to heat.
Toss in shallots and stir and cook for 5 minutes.
Stir in garlic paste and cook for 1 minute.
Transfer it to the slow cooker, greased with cooking spray.
Place brisket in the same pan and sear until golden from both sides.
Transfer the beef to the slow cooker along with other ingredients except for cheese.
Put on its lid and cook for 8 hrs. on low heat.
Garnish with cheese and serve.

NUTRITION: Calories 397, Protein 25g, Fat 34g, Carbs 9g, Fiber 0 g

Veggie Tacos with Coconut Aminos

Prep Time: 10 minutes   **Cook time:** 25 minutes   **Serves** 4

Ingredients:
Veggie tacos
1 tablespoon extravirgin olive oil
1 red bell pepper, chopped
½ small onion, chopped
½ cup sugarfree ketchup
1 tablespoon powdered monk fruit sweetener
1 tablespoon coconut aminos
1 teaspoon yellow mustard
2 Keto Bagels, for serving

Directions:
Prepare the cauliflowerpecan taco "meat" as directed in the veggie tacos recipe. (Omit the lettuce leaves.)
In a large nonstick skillet, heat the olive oil until hot. Add the bell pepper and onion and sauté for 3 minutes, or until the veggies are soft.
Stir in the taco "meat" and stir to combine. Cook for 5 minutes to warm the mixture through.
In a small bowl, combine the ketchup, monk fruit sweetener, coconut aminos, and mustard.
Add the ketchup mixture to the sloppy joe mixture and stir to combine.
Add ¼ cup water if the mixture seems too thick.
Serve on top of a toasted keto bagel half if desired.

NUTRITION: Calories: 344 Fat: 28g Protein: 7g Total Carbs: 16g Fiber: 7g Net Carbs: 9g

Italian Squash Soup

Prep time: 10 minutes. **Cook time:** 15 minutes. **Serves:** 4

Ingredients:
3 tablespoons extra-virgin olive oil
1 small red onion, sliced
1 garlic clove, minced
1 cup shredded zucchini
1 cup shredded yellow squash
½ cup shredded carrot
3 cups vegetable broth
1 teaspoon salt
2 tablespoons chopped fresh basil
1 tablespoon chopped fresh chives
2 tablespoons pine nuts

Directions:
In a suitable pot, heat the oil over high heat.

Add the onion and garlic and sauté until softened, 5 to 7 minutes.

Add the zucchini, yellow squash, and carrot and sauté until softened, 1 to 2 minutes.

Add the broth and salt and bring to a boil.

Reduce its heat to a simmer and cook until the vegetables are soft, 1 to 2 minutes.

Stir in the basil and chives and serve, sprinkled with the pine nuts.

NUTRITION: Calories 173; Fat 16g; Sodium 1167mg; Carbs 7g; Fiber 2g; Sugars 1g; Protein 5g

Tender Lamb

Prep time: 2 hours **Cooking time:** 2 hours and 5 minutes **Servings:** 6

A powerhouse of many nutritional benefits, including anti-inflammatory properties and more protein than meat and chicken

Ingredients

3 lamb shanks

Seasoning mixture (1 tbsp. oregano, ¼ tsp. cumin, ground, and 1 tbsp. paprika, smoked)

3 garlic cloves, minced

2 C. red wine

4 C. beef stock

Directions

Coat the lamb shanks with the seasoning mixture, and sprinkle with salt and pepper.

Cover with minced garlic and marinate in half of the mixture for 30 minutes.

Set the instant pot to sauté, add 2 tbsp. of olive oil and brown the lamb on all sides. Remove and set aside.

Add the rest of the ingredients to the pot, return the lamb and cover it.

Set it to manual to cook at high pressure for 30 minutes.

Release the pressure naturally, remove, and make the sauce.

Set the instant pot to sauté to simmer and thicken the sauce.

NUTRITION: Calories: 391 kcal Total Fat: 20.46 g Saturated Fat: 77 g Cholesterol: 100.5 mg Sodium: 4905 mg Total Carbohydrates: 61 g Dietary Fiber: 0.42 g Total Sugar: 54 g Protein: 33 g Potassium: 8154 mg.

Quick Hummus Recipe

Time: 10 minutes **Serving Size:** 1 ½ cup **Prep Time: 10 minutes Cook Time:** 0 minutes

Traditional hummus uses chickpeas, but you can get creative and try substituting the chickpeas with other variants such as white, black, or pinto beans.

Ingredients:

1 ½ cup chickpeas, boiled until tender (or a 15 ounce can of chickpeas)

¼ cup tahini

¼ cup lemon juice

2 cloves of garlic, finely minced

30 ml olive oil (choose a good brand of the extra virgin kind)
½ tsp salt to taste
½ tsp cumin powder
Water

Directions:
Using a food processor, make sure to incorporate the lemon juice and tahini. Mix for about a minute until smooth.
Then add salt, cumin and garlic, and mix again for 30 seconds.
Scrape down the sides and mix 1 more time for 30 seconds.
Next, drain the chickpeas, add some to the mix and blend again for 1 minute. Scrape down the sides once more, add more chickpeas, and blend. Continue this process until you have used all of the chickpeas. At this point, the mix will look grainy or dry; therefore, you can add half a tablespoon of water and blend again. Add more water until you end up with a silky smooth paste. Check for salt, and adjust if necessary.
Keep hummus in an air-tight container in your fridge.
Greek Yogurt
A good anti-inflammation probiotic to have in your fridge, Greek yogurt is not only a great aid for cooking various recipes, but doubles as a quick snack.
Pair your yogurt with healthy options like berries. Have about 3–4 varieties of berries stored, so you can pop them in a cup of yogurt to enjoy whenever
you need a snack or a sweet treat.
Nuts and Nut Butters
Nuts make great healthy snacks for any diet. They are rich in omega-3
essential oils and provide fiber, protein, and antioxidative values together with plenty of vitamins and minerals. Good choices include:
Almonds
Pistachios
Walnuts
Pecans
Peanuts
Hazelnuts
Similar to the whole nuts, natural nut butter makes a good snack, as well as a breakfast accompaniment. As a snack, you can use a nut butter spread on celery, slices of apple or pears. Experiment with your favorite nut butter, and find your all-time favorite snack. A word of caution, though: Nut butter can be high in calories. Plus, make sure to purchase the natural varieties, minus the additives.

NUTRITION: Calories 190 Carbs18 g Fat11 g Protein 6 g Fiber 5 g

Ginger-Cilantro Turkey Burgers

Prep time: 10 minutes   **Cook time:** 10 minutes   **Serves** 4

Ingredients:
1½ pounds (680 g) ground turkey
1 large egg, lightly beaten
2 tablespoons coconut flour (or almond flour) ½ cup finely chopped onion
1 garlic clove, minced

2 teaspoons minced fresh ginger root
1 tablespoon fresh cilantro
1 teaspoon salt
¼ teaspoon freshly ground black pepper
1 tablespoon extra-virgin olive oil

Directions:

In a medium bowl, combine the ground turkey, egg, flour, onion, garlic, ginger root, cilantro, salt, and pepper and mix well.
Form the turkey mixture into four patties.
Heat the olive oil in a large skillet over medium-high heat.
Cook the burgers, flipping once, until firm to the touch, 3 to 4 minutes on each side. Serve.

NUTRITION: calories: 320 fat: 20g protein: 34g carbs: 2g fiber: 1g sugar: 1g sodium: 720mg

Spinach Berry with Bacon Salad

Prep time: 10 minutes **Cook time:** 10 minutes **Serves** 4

Ingredients:
3 slices bacon
1 garlic clove, minced
3 cups baby spinach
½ cup strawberries, trimmed and halved
½ avocado, pitted, peeled, and diced
2 tablespoons Balsamic Vinaigrette

Directions:
In a large skillet, cook the bacon over medium heat for about 10 minutes, or until crisp. Transfer to a paper towel–lined plate. Coarsely chop the cooked bacon slices.
Put the spinach, strawberries, avocado, and bacon in a large salad bowl.
Drizzle with the dressing just before serving and toss to combine. Enjoy immediately.

NUTRITION: Calories: 463 Fat: 34g Protein: 18g Total Carbs: 26g Fiber: 12g Net Carbs: 14g

Mediterranean Poached Cod

Prep time: 15 minutes. **Cook time:** 25 minutes. **Serves:** 4

Ingredients:
1 pound cod fillet, cut into 4 equal pieces
1 teaspoon salt
½ teaspoon black pepper
½ cup extra-virgin olive oil
1 red bell pepper, sliced
1 (14-ounce) can artichoke hearts, drained and quartered 1 (6-ounce) can large pitted green or black olives, drained and halved 4 large garlic cloves, peeled and crushed
2 tablespoons chopped fresh rosemary, or 2 teaspoons dried ¼ cup white wine vinegar or rice vinegar

Directions:

Sprinkle the cod with black pepper and salt.

In a suitable skillet, heat 2 tablespoons of olive oil over medium-high heat.

Sear the cod for almost 1 to 2 minutes per side. Transfer the fish to a serving dish and keep warm.

In the same skillet, add the rest of the 6 tablespoons of olive oil over medium heat. Add the bell pepper, artichokes, olives, garlic, and rosemary and sauté for almost 2 to 3 minutes until very fragrant.

Reduce its heat to low, stir in the vinegar, return the cod to this skillet, cover and poach for almost 10 to 12 minutes, until the fish is cooked through and the vegetables are tender.

Serve the cod and vegetables warm, drizzled with the cooking oil.

NUTRITION: Calories 419; Fat 31g; Sodium 1118mg; Carbs 16.6g; Fiber 7.3g; Sugars 2.6g; Protein 24.1g

Swordfish with Pineapple and Cilantro

Prep Time: 12-minutes   **Total time:** 32-minutes   **Yield:** 4-servings

Ingredients:

1 tsp. Salt.
1 tbsp. coconut aminos
¼ c. chopped fresh cilantro
2 minced garlic cloves
¼ tsp. Ground black pepper.
2 tbsps. Chopped fresh parsley
2 lbs. sliced swordfish
1 tbsp. coconut oil
1 c. fresh pineapple chunks

Directions:

Preheat the oven to 400F. Grease a baking tray with coconut oil. Mix cilantro, coconut aminos, garlic, pineapple, parsley, pepper, swordfish, and salt. Set the dish to the oven and allow it to bake for about 20-minutes.

NUTRITION: Calories: 444 Protein: 47.53 g Fat: 20.32
carbohydrates: 16.44 g

Mango & Coconut Rice Pudding

Servings: 4 **Cooking Time**: 25 Minutes

Ingredients:

1 can coconut milk
1 mango, sliced
¼ cup caster sugar
1 tsp ground ginger
A pinch of sea salt
2 cups cooked brown rice

Directions:

1. Place the sugar, ginger, and salt in a pot over medium heat and cook for 3-4 minutes until the sugar dissolves. Mix in brown rice and cook for another 3 minutes until the rice is heated through. Spoon into serving bowls and top with the sliced mango. Serve and enjoy!

Healthy Pasta Salad

Servings: 6 **Cooking Time:** 10 Minutes

Ingredients:
1 package of glutenfree fusilli pasta
1 cup of grape tomatoes, sliced
1 handful of fresh cilantro, chopped
1 cup of olives, halved
1 cup of fresh basil, chopped
½ cup of olive oil
Sea salt to taste

Directions:
1. Whisk together the olive oil, chopped basil, cilantro, and sea salt. Set aside.
2. Cook the pasta according to package directions, strain, and rinse.
3. Combine the pasta with the tomatoes and olives.
4. Add the olive oil mixture, and toss until well combined.

NUTRITION: Total Carbohydrates 66g Dietary Fiber: 5g Protein: 13g Total Fat: 23g Calories: 525

Ground Meat Stroganoff

Ingredients:
1 lb lean ground meat
1 little onion diced
1 clove garlic minced
3/4 lb new mushrooms cut
3 tablespoons flour
2 cups meat stock
salt and pepper to taste
2 teaspoons Worcestershire sauce
3/4 cup sharp cream
2 tablespoons new parsley

Directions:
1. Dark colored ground hamburger, onion and garlic (making an effort not to split it up something over the top) in a dish until no pink remains. Channel fat.
2. Include cut mushrooms and cook 23 minutes. Mix in flour and cook 1 progressively minute.
3. Include stock, Worcestershire sauce, salt and pepper and heat to the point of boiling. Lessen warmth and stew on low 10 minutes. Cook egg noodles as indicated by bundle headings.
4. Expel meat blend from the warmth, mix in sharp cream and parsley.
5. Serve over egg noodles.

Chicken And Glutenfree Noodle Soup

Servings: 4 **Cooking Time**: 25 Minutes

Ingredients:

¼ cup extravirgin olive oil
3 celery stalks, cut into
¼inch slices 2 medium carrots, cut into
¼inch dice 1 small onion, cut into
¼inch dice 1 fresh rosemary sprig
4 cups chicken broth
8 ounces glutenfree penne
1 teaspoon salt
¼ teaspoon freshly ground black pepper
2 cups diced rotisserie chicken
¼ cup finely chopped fresh flatleaf parsley

Directions:

1. Heatup the oil over high heat in a large pot.
2. Put the celery, carrots, onion, and rosemary and sauté until softened, 5 to 7 minutes.
3. Add the broth, penne, salt, and pepper and boil.
4. Simmer and cook until the penne is tender, 8 to 10 minutes.
5. Remove and discard the rosemary sprig, and add the chicken and parsley.
6. Reduce the heat to low. Cook within 5 minutes, and serve.

NUTRITION: Calories 485 Total Fat: 18g Total Carbohydrates: 47g Sugar: 4g Fiber: 7g Protein: 33g Sodium: 1423mg

Chicken And Snap Pea Stirfry

Servings: 4 **Cooking Time**: 10 Minutes

Ingredients:

1 ¼ cups boneless skinless chicken breast, thinly sliced
3 tablespoons fresh cilantro, chopped
2 tablespoons vegetable oil
2 tablespoons of sesame seeds
1 bunch scallions, thinly sliced
2 teaspoons Sriracha
2 garlic cloves, minced
2 tablespoons rice vinegar
1 bell pepper, thinly sliced
3 tablespoons soy sauce
2½ cups snap peas
Salt, to taste
Freshly ground black pepper, to taste

Directions:

1. Heatup the oil in a pan over medium heat. Add garlic and thinly sliced scallions.
Cook for a minute and then add 2 ½ cups snap peas along with bell pepper. Cook until tender, just for about 34 minutes.
2. Add chicken and cook for about 45 minutes, or until thoroughly cooked.

3. Add in 2 teaspoons Sriracha, 2 tablespoons of sesame seeds, 3 tablespoons soy sauce, and 2 tablespoons rice vinegar. Toss everything until wellcombined. Simmer within 23 minutes over low heat.
4. Add 3 tablespoons of chopped cilantro and stir well. Transfer, and sprinkle with extra sesame seeds and cilantro, if needed. Enjoy!

NUTRITION: 228 calories 11 g fat 11 g total carbs 20 g protein

Shiitake And Spinach Pattie

Servings: 8 **Cooking Time**: 15 Minutes

Ingredients:
1 ½ cups shiitake mushrooms, minced
1 ½ cups spinach, chopped
3 garlic cloves, minced
2 onions, minced
4 teaspoon olive oil
1 egg
1 ½ cups quinoa, cooked
1 ½ teaspoon Italian seasoning
1/3 cup toasted sunflower seeds, ground
1/3 cup Pecorino cheese, grated

Directions:
1. Heat olive oil in a saucepan. Once hot, sauté shiitake mushrooms for 3 minutes or until lightly seared. Add in garlic and onion. Sauté for 2 minutes or until fragrant and translucent. Set aside.
2. In the same saucepan, heat the remaining olive oil. Add in spinach. Reduce heat, then simmer for 1 minute, drain and transfer to a strainer.
3. Chop spinach finely and add into the mushroom mixture. Add egg into the spinach mixture. Fold in cooked quinoa—season with Italian seasoning, then mix until well combined. Sprinkle sunflower seeds and cheese.
4. Divide the spinach mixture into patties—Cook patties within 5 minutes or until firm and golden brown. Serve with burger bread.

NUTRITION: Calories 43 Carbs: 9g Fat: 0g Protein: 3g

Chicken Salad With Chinese Touch

Servings: 3 **Cooking Time**: 25 Minutes

Ingredients:
1 Medium green onion (thinly sliced)
2 Boneless chicken breasts
2 tablespoon Soya sauce
¼ Teaspoon white pepper
1 tablespoon sesame oil
4 cups romaine lettuce (chopped)
1 cup cabbage (shredded)
¼ Cup small cubes carrots
¼ Cup thin sliced almonds
¼ Cup noodles (only for serving)

For Preparing Chinese Dressing:
 1 Minced garlic clove
 1 Teaspoon soy sauce
 1 tablespoon sesame oil
 2 tablespoon Rice vinegar
 1 tablespoon Sugar

Directions:
1. Prepare Chinese dressing by whisking all ingredients in a bowl.
2. In a bowl, marinate chicken breasts with garlic, olive oil, soy sauce, and white pepper for 20 minutes.
3. Place baking dish in the preheated oven (at 225C).
4. Place chicken breasts in the baking dish and bake it almost for 20 minutes.
5. For assembling the salad, combine romaine lettuce, cabbage, carrots, and green onion.
6. For serving, place a chicken piece in a plate and salad on top of it. Pour some dressing over it alongside noodles.

NUTRITION: Calories 130 Carbs: 10g Fat: 6g Protein: 10g

Crispy Cheesecrusted Fish Fillet

Servings: 4 **Cooking Time:** 10 Minutes

Ingredients:
¼cup wholewheat breadcrumbs
¼cup Parmesan cheese, grated
¼teaspoon sea salt
¼teaspoon ground pepper
1Tablespoon olive oil
4pcs tilapia fillets

Directions:
1. Preheat the oven to 375°F.
2. Stir in the breadcrumbs, Parmesan cheese, salt, pepper, and olive oil in a mixing bowl.
3. Mix well until blended thoroughly.
4. Coat the fillets with the mixture, and lay each on a lightly sprayed baking sheet.
5. Place the sheet in the oven.
6. Bake for 10 minutes until the fillets cook through and turn brownish.

NUTRITION: Calories: 255Fat: 7gProtein: 15.9gCarbs: 34gFiber: 2.6g

Spiced Garlicky Chicken Sauté

Prep time: 10 minutes **Cook time:** 15 minutes **Serves** 4

Ingredients:
3 tablespoons extra-virgin olive oil
1 red bell pepper, chopped
1 onion, chopped
1½ pounds boneless, skinless chicken breasts, cut into bite-size pieces 5 garlic cloves, minced
½ teaspoon sea salt
¼ teaspoon freshly ground black pepper

Directions:
1. In a large nonstick skillet over medium-high heat, heat the olive oil until it shimmers.
2. Add the red bell pepper, onion, and chicken. Cook for 10 minutes, stirring it occasionally.
3. Add the garlic, salt, and pepper. Cook for 30 seconds, stirring constantly.

NUTRITION: Calories: 179 Fat: 13g Protein: 10g Total Carbs: 6g Fiber: 1g Net Carbs: 5g

Spiced Rosemary Chicken

Prep time: 5 minutes **Cook time:** 20 minutes **Serves** 4

Ingredients:
1½ pounds chicken breast tenders
2 tablespoons extra-virgin olive oil
2 tablespoons chopped fresh rosemary leaves
½ teaspoon sea salt
⅛ teaspoon freshly ground black pepper

Directions:
1. Preheat the oven to 425°F.
2. Place the chicken tenders on a rimmed baking sheet. Brush them with the olive oil and sprinkle with the rosemary, salt, and pepper.
3. Bake for 15 to 20 minutes, or until the juices run clear.

NUTRITION: Calories: 389 Fat: 20g Protein: 49g Total Carbs: 2g Fiber: 1g Net Carbs: 1g

Garlick and Onion Turkey Meatballs

Prep time: 10 minutes **Cook time:** 10 minutes **Serves** 4

Ingredients:
1½ pounds ground turkey
1 cup shredded cabbage
¼ cup chopped fresh cilantro leaves
1 tablespoon grated fresh ginger
1 teaspoon garlic powder
1 teaspoon onion powder
½ teaspoon sea salt
⅛ teaspoon freshly ground black pepper
2 tablespoons olive oil

Directions:
1. In a large bowl, combine the turkey, cabbage, cilantro, ginger, garlic powder, onion powder, salt, and pepper. Mix well. Form the turkey mixture into about 20 (¾-inch) meatballs.
2. In a large nonstick skillet over medium-high heat, heat the olive oil until it shimmers.
3. Add the meatballs and cook for about 10 minutes, turning as they brown.

NUTRITION: Calories: 408 Fat: 26g Protein: 47g Total Carbs: 4g Fiber: 1g Net Carbs: 3g

Turkey and Kale Sauté

Prep time: 10 minutes **Cook time:** 10 minutes **Serves** 4

Ingredients:
2 tablespoons extra-virgin olive oil
1½ pounds ground turkey breast
2 cups stemmed and chopped kale
½ onion, chopped
2 tablespoons fresh thyme leaves
½ teaspoon sea salt
⅛ teaspoon freshly ground black pepper
5 garlic cloves, minced

1. In a large nonstick skillet over medium-high heat, heat the olive oil until it shimmers.
2. Add the turkey, kale, onion, thyme, salt, and pepper. Cook for about 5 minutes, crumbling the turkey with a spoon until it browns.
3. Add the garlic. Cook for 30 seconds, stirring constantly.

NUTRITION: Calories: 413 Fat: 20g Protein: 50g Total Carbs: 7g Fiber: 1g Net Carbs: 6g

Rosemary with Spiced Turkey

Prep time: 10 minutes **Cook time:** 10 minutes **Serves** 4

Ingredients:
3 tablespoons extra-virgin olive oil
2 red bell peppers, chopped
1 onion, chopped
1½ pounds boneless, skinless turkey breasts, cut into bite-size pieces 2 tablespoons chopped fresh rosemary leaves
½ teaspoon sea salt
⅛ teaspoon freshly ground black pepper
3 garlic cloves, minced

Directions:
1. In a large nonstick skillet over medium-high heat, heat the olive oil until it shimmers.
2. Add the red bell peppers, onion, turkey, rosemary, salt, and pepper. Cook for 7 to 10 minutes, stirring occasionally, until the turkey is cooked and the vegetables are tender.
3. Add the garlic. Cook for 30 seconds more, stirring constantly.

NUTRITION: Calories: 303 Fat: 14g Protein: 30g Total Carbs: 15g Fiber: 2g Net Carbs: 13g

Garlicky Parsley with Pork Tenderloin

Prep time: 10 minutes Cook time: 15 minutes Serves 4

Ingredients:
½ cup fresh parsley leaves
¼ cup Dijon mustard
6 garlic cloves

3 tablespoons fresh rosemary leaves
3 tablespoons extra-virgin olive oil
½ teaspoon sea salt
¼ teaspoon freshly ground black pepper
1 (1½-pound) pork tenderloin

Directions:
1. Preheat the oven to 400°F.
2. In a blender or food processor, combine the parsley, mustard, garlic, rosemary, olive oil, salt, and pepper. Pulse in 1-second pulses, about 20
times, until a paste forms. Rub this paste all over the tenderloin and put the pork on a rimmed baking sheet.
3. Bake the pork for about 15 minutes, or until it registers 165°F on an instant-read meat thermometer.
4. Let rest for 5 minutes, slice, and serve.

NUTRITION: Calories: 362 Fat: 18g Protein: 2g Total Carbs: 5g Fiber: 2g Net Carbs: 3g

Mustardy Pork Chops with Kale

Prep time: 10 minutes **Cook time:** 15 minutes **Serves** 4

Ingredients:
4 thin-cut pork chops
1 teaspoon sea salt, divided
¼ teaspoon freshly ground black pepper, divided
4 tablespoons Dijon mustard, divided
3 tablespoons extra-virgin olive oil
½ red onion, finely chopped
4 cups stemmed and chopped kale
2 tablespoons apple cider vinegar

Directions:
1. Preheat the oven to 425°F.
2. Season the pork chops with ½ teaspoon of the salt and ⅛ teaspoon of the pepper. Spread 2 tablespoons of the mustard over them and put them on a rimmed baking sheet. Bake for about 15 minutes, or until the pork registers an internal temperature of 165°F on an instant-read meat thermometer.
3. While the pork cooks, in a large nonstick skillet over medium-high, heat the olive oil until it shimmers.
4. Add the red onion and kale. Cook for about 7 minutes, stirring occasionally, until the vegetables soften.
5. In a small bowl, whisk the remaining 2 tablespoons of mustard, the cider vinegar, the remaining ½ teaspoon of salt, and the remaining ⅛ teaspoon of pepper. Add this to the kale. Cook for 2 minutes, stirring.

NUTRITION: Calories: 504 Fat: 39g Protein: 28g Total Carbs: 10g Fiber: 2g Net Carbs: 8g

Berry Sauce with Beef Tenderloin

Prep time: 10 minutes **Cook time:** 15 minutes **Serves** 4

Ingredients:
4 beef tenderloin filets, about ¾ inch thick

1 teaspoon sea salt, divided
¼ teaspoon freshly ground black pepper, divided
2 tablespoons extra-virgin olive oil
1 shallot, finely minced
½ cup tawny port
2 cups fresh blueberries
3 tablespoons very cold butter, cut into pieces

Directions:
1. Season the beef with ½ teaspoon of the salt and ⅛ teaspoon of the pepper.
2. In a large skillet over medium-high heat, heat the olive oil until it shimmers.
3. Add the seasoned steaks. Cook for about 5 minutes per side, or until the beef registers an internal temperature of 130°F on an instant-read meat thermometer. Set aside on a platter, tented with aluminum foil.
4. Return the skillet to the heat. Add the shallot, port, blueberries, and the remaining ½ teaspoon of salt, and the remaining ⅛ teaspoon of pepper.
Use a wooden spoon to scrape any browned bits from the bottom of the pan. Bring to a simmer and reduce the heat to medium-low. Simmer for about 4 minutes, stirring and smashing the blueberries slightly, until the liquid reduces by half.
5. One piece at a time, whisk in the butter. Return the meat to the skillet.
Turn it once to coat with the sauce. Serve with the remaining sauce spooned over the meat.

NUTRITION: Calories: 554 Fat: 32g Protein: 50g Total Carbs: 14g Fiber: 2g Net Carbs: 12g

Almond & Chia Bites With Cherries
Servings: 2 **Cooking Time**: 20 Minutes

Ingredients:
1 cup cherries, pitted
1 cup shredded coconut
¼ cup chia seeds
¾ cup ground almonds
¼ cup cocoa nibs

Directions:
1. Blend cherries, coconut, chia seeds, almonds, and cocoa nibs in a food processor until crumbly. Shape the mixture into 24 balls and arrange on a lined baking sheet. Let sit in the fridge for 15 minutes. Serve and enjoy!

NUTRITION:
Per Serving: Calories: 95;Fat: 2g;Protein: 4g;Carbs: 22g.

Impressive Parfait With Yogurt, Berry, And Walnut
Servings: 2 **Cooking Time:** 0 Minutes

Ingredients:

2 cups plain unsweetened yogurt, or plain unsweetened coconut yogurt or almond yogurt
2 tablespoons honey
1 cup blueberries, fresh
1 cup raspberries, fresh
½ cup walnut pieces

Directions:

1. Whisk the yogurt and honey in a medium bowl. Spoon into 2 serving bowls.
2. Top each with ½ cup blueberries, ½ cup raspberries, and ¼ cup walnut pieces.

NUTRITION: Per Serving: Calories: 505 ;Fat: 22g ;Protein: 23g ;Carbs: 56g .

Quinoa & Spinach Salad

Prep time: 10 minutes. **Cooking time:** 0 minutes. **Servings:** 2

Ingredients:

16 ounces quinoa, cooked
1 handful raisins
1 handful baby spinach leaves
1 tablespoon maple syrup
½ tablespoon lemon juice
½ Tablespoon olive oil
1 teaspoon ground cumin
Sea salt and black pepper, a pinch
½ teaspoon chili flakes

Directions:

1. Toss the quinoa with spinach, raisins, cumin, salt, and pepper in a mixing bowl. Toss in the maple syrup, lemon juice, oil, and chili flakes, then serve as a breakfast side dish.
2. Enjoy!

NUTRITION: Calories: 170 Fat: 3 g Fiber: 6 g Carbs: 8 g Protein: 5 g

Winter Style Fruit Salad

Servings: 6 Cooking Time: 0 Minutes

Ingredients:

- 4 cooked sweet potatoes, cubed (1-inch cubes) 3 pears, cubed (1-inch cubes)
- 1 cup of grapes, halved
- 1 apple, cubed
- ½ cup of pecan halves
- 2 tablespoons of olive oil
- 1 tablespoon of red wine vinegar
- 2 tablespoons of raw honey

Directions:

1. Mix the olive oil, red wine vinegar, then the raw honey to make the dressing, and set aside.
2. Combine the chopped fruit, sweet potato, and pecan halves, and divide this between six serving bowls. Drizzle each bowl with the dressing.

NUTRITION: Total Carbohydrates 40g Dietary Fiber: 6g Protein: 3g Total Fat: 11g Calories: 251

Limey Cilantro with Shrimp Salad

Prep time: 10 minutes   **Cook time:** 5 minutes   **Serves** 1

Ingredients:
6 ounces shrimp, peeled and deveined
2 cups mixed greens
1 avocado, pitted, peeled, and diced
1 scallion, finely sliced
¼ cup Cilantro Lime Vinaigrette

Directions:
Fill a small pot with filtered water and bring to a boil. Add the shrimp and cook for 2 or 3 minutes, until they turn pink and become opaque. Using a strainer, drain the shrimp and immediately rinse under cold running water until they're cool to touch.
Put the mixed greens in a salad bowl. Top with the avocado, scallions, and cooked shrimp.
Drizzle the dressing onto the salad and toss to combine. Enjoy right away.

NUTRITION: Calories: 629   Fat: 47g   Protein: 32g   Total Carbs: 31g   Fiber: 19g   Net Carbs: 12g

Snow Pea and Watermelon Salad

Prep time: 25 minutes   **Cook time:** 0 minutes   **Serves** 4

Dressing:
½ cup olive oil
¼ cup apple cider vinegar
2 tablespoons raw honey
1 teaspoon freshly grated lemon zest (optional) Pinch sea salt
Salad:
4 cups (½-inch) watermelon cubes
1 English cucumber, cut into ½-inch cubes
1 cup halved snow peas
1 scallion, white and green parts, chopped
2 cups shredded kale
1 tablespoon chopped fresh cilantro

Make the Dressing
In a small bowl, whisk the olive oil, cider vinegar, honey, and lemon zest (if using). Season with sea salt and set it aside.

Make the Salad
In a large bowl, toss together the watermelon, cucumber, snow peas, scallion, and dressing.
Divide the kale among four plates and top with the watermelon mixture.
Serve garnished with the cilantro.

NUTRITION: calories: 353   fat: 26g   protein: 4g   carbs: 30g   fiber: 3g   sugar: 20g sodium: 8mg

Anti-Inflammatory Fruit Salad

Prep time: 10 minutes **Cooking Time**: 25 minutes **Servings**: 4

Ingredients:

3 apples
2 pears
1 cup blueberries
1 tablespoon ground ginger
½ teaspoon cinnamon
3 tablespoons water
1 tablespoon honey

Directions:

Peel the apples and pears.
Chop the fruit into the medium pieces and transfer them to a tray.
Wash the blueberries carefully and put them in a blender.
Blend the berries until smooth.
Add the honey, water, ground ginger, and cinnamon.
Blend the mixture for 1 minute more on high speed.
Sprinkle the chopped fruits with the blueberry mixture and mix up the dish carefully.
Preheat the oven to 350 F.
Cover the fruit with the foil and transfer it to the oven.
Bake the dish for 25 minutes.
Remove the fruit from the oven and cool slightly.
Serve the dish warm.

NUTRITION: Calories: 199Fat: 6 gTotal Carbs: 52g Sugars: 40g Protein: 1g

Swiss Chard and Egg Salad

Prep time: 25 minutes   **Cook time**: 0 minutes **Serves** 4

Dressing:

¼ cup olive oil
3 tablespoons freshly squeezed lemon juice
2 teaspoons raw honey
1 teaspoon Dijon mustard
Sea salt, to taste

Salad:

5 cups chopped Swiss chard
3 large hard-boiled eggs, peeled and chopped
1 English cucumber, diced
½ cup sliced radishes
½ cup chopped pecans

For the Dressing

In a small bowl, whisk the olive oil, lemon juice, honey, and mustard.
Season with salt and set it aside.

For the Salad

In a large bowl, toss the Swiss chard and dressing together for about 4 minutes, or until the greens start to soften. Divide the greens evenly among four plates. Top each salad with egg, cucumber, radishes, and pecans.

NUTRITION: calories: 241 fat: 21g protein: 7g carbs: 9g fiber: 2g sugar: 5g sodium: 163mg

Orange Chicken Salad

Prep time: 10 minutes. **Cooking time:** 30 minutes. **Servings**: 4

Ingredients:

1 whole chicken, cut into medium pieces
2 Scallions, chopped
2 Celery ribs, chopped
1 cup chopped mandarin orange
¼ cup avocado mayonnaise
½ cup coconut cream
1 cup chopped cashews, toasted
A pinch of salt and black pepper

Directions:

Put chicken pieces in a pot and add water to cover. Add a pinch of salt, then bring to a boil over medium heat and cook for 25 minutes. Transfer to a cutting board, discard bones, shred meat, and put in a bowl. Add celery, orange pieces, cashews, scallion, salt, pepper, mayo, and coconut cream, toss to coat, and serve.
Enjoy!

NUTRITION: Calories: 210 Fat: 3 g Fiber: 3 g arbs: 16 g Protein: 18 g

Chickpea Salad

Prep time: 15 minutes. **Cook time:** 20 minutes. **Serves:** 4

Ingredients:

1 small acorn squash, seeded and sliced
1 cup sliced carrots
½ cup sliced parsnips
½ small red onion, sliced
3 tablespoons extra-virgin olive oil
1 garlic clove, minced
1 teaspoon salt
¼ teaspoon black pepper, freshly ground
1 (15-ounce) can chickpeas, drained and rinsed 2 cups baby arugula
1 tablespoon apple cider vinegar

Directions:

At 400 degrees F, preheat your oven.

In a 9-by-13-inch casserole dish, toss together the squash, carrots, parsnips, onion, oil, garlic, salt, and pepper until well mixed.

Transfer the dish to the oven, and roast until the vegetables are golden brown and tender, 15 to 20 min. Remove from the oven and let cool to room temperature.

Add the chickpeas, arugula, and vinegar, toss to combine, and serve.

NUTRITION: Calories 349; Fat 14g; Sodium 421mg; Carbs 50.2g; Fiber 19g; Sugars 4g; Protein 14g

Cucumber and Bulgur Salad

Prep time: 15 minutes.   **Cook time**: 10 minutes.   **Serves**: 4

Ingredients:

½ cup bulgur

1 ½ cups water

¾ teaspoon salt

2 tablespoons lemon juice

3 tablespoons extra-virgin olive oil

1 cup medium diced tomato

1 cup medium diced cucumber

⅓ cup chopped fresh parsley

Directions:

In a small saucepan over medium-high heat, combine bulgur, water, and ¼ teaspoon salt. Bring to a boil. Then cover, reduce heat to simmer, and cook 10 minutes. Turn off heat and let sit, covered, another 5 minutes.

Drain off any excess liquid, fluff bulgur with a fork, and place in a serving bowl, letting it come to room temperature while preparing rest of salad.

In a suitable bowl, whisk together lemon juice, oil, and remaining ½ teaspoon salt.

Add tomato, cucumber, and parsley to the bowl with bulgur. Add dressing, toss well to combine, and serve.

NUTRITION: Calories 164; Fat 9g; Sodium 450mg; Carbs 16g; Fiber 4g; Sugars 7g; Protein 8g

21 Day Meal Plan

B. Breakfast *L.* Lunch *D.* Dinner

Day 1	Day 2	Day 3	Day 4
B. Quick Burrito L. Green Soup D. Salmon Balls	B.Beef Breakfast L. Edamame Omelet D. LemonHerb Tilapia	B. Eggs With Cheese L. Lentils with Tomatoes **D.** Curry Pork Mix	B. Golden Milk L. Grilled Chicken D. Beef, Pork, and Lamb
Day 5	**Day 6**	**Day 7**	**Day 8**
B. Milk and Creamy Yogurt Bowl L. Bean Shawaema Salad D. Chickpea Curry	B. Orange Oatmeal Muffins L. Lettuce Wraps D. Meatballs	B. Strawberry & Pecan L. Balsamic Chicken D. Rosemary Pork Chops	B. Avocado Egg L. Cod and Quinoa Mix D. Aromatic Turkey
Day 9	**Day 10**	**Day 11**	**Day 12**
B. Papaya Breakfast L. Quick Pumpkin Soup D. Lemony Salmon	B. Sweet Potato L. Green Soup D. Beef Pork and Lamb	B.Chia Pudding L. Balsamic Chicken and Vegetables D. Mushroom Risotto	B. Crepes L. Jicama Black Bean D. Spicy Ramen Soup
Day 13	**Day 14**	**Day 15**	**Day 16**
B. Quick Burrito L. Cherrybalsamic Chicken Breasts D. Balsamic Chicken	B. Golden Milk L. Edamame Omelet D. Salmon and Feta Cheese en Papillote	B. Coconut Cancakes L. Edamame Omelet D. Curry Pork Mix	B. Fruit and Millet L. Capellini Soup D. Mushroom Risotto
Day 17	**Day 18**	**Day 19**	**Day 20**
B. Breakfast Salad L. Bean Shawarma Salad D. Salmon Balls	B. Blueberry Breakfast Blend L. Lettuce Wraps D. Beef, Pork, and Lamb	B. Eggs With Cheese L. Beets Gazpacho D. New England Clam Chow	B. Walnut Bowl L. Green Soup D. Rosemary Pork Chops
Day 21			
B. Papaya Breakfast L. Capocollo and Garlic Chicken D. Meatballs			